THE 180° THEORY

How to become mentally self-sufficient

Dr. Robert O. Nara
& Steven Mariner

The 180° Theory

—How to Become Mentally Self-Sufficient

by Dr. Robert O. Nara
and Steven A. Mariner

Published by
ORAMEDICS INTERNATIONAL PRESS
200 East Montezuma Avenue
Houghton, Michigan 49931

Library of Congress
Catalog Card Number: 79—90866

ISBN: 0-933420-02-1

First Printing: October 1979

Printed in U.S.A.

Table of Contents

A Friend
leaves all of your freedoms intact
but obliges you to be fully all you are
and helps you to become all you can be...

Introduction

The wind came gently from the north, its fingers picking fitfully at the corners of the flags draped over the bodies of five airmen. The wind had been their only companion for nearly 17 years; it was offering its last, reluctant farewell before these men finally began their journey home to the United States.

Those preparing to load the sun-bleached bones aboard the waiting transport spoke in hushed tones. Some of them wept. They were the first to begin piecing together the 17-year mystery of the lost B-24 bomber, *Lady Be Good.* They were standing in the midst of evidence of extraordinary courage and achievement...and of enormous error and tragic futility.

Eighty miles away, across the sand-dunes and the sun blasted plateau, deep in the Libyan Sahara, the *Lady Be Good* patiently waited for her crewmen to return. She is still there, in that trackless hell where men never venture and even birds unfortunate enough to visit cannot leave...The 125 degree temperature bakes even the atmosphere; it is so thin no bird would have the strength to become airborne. The desert nomads believe the plateau is cursed by Allah; they won't go there.

It belongs to the *Lady Be Good*, and she'll be there forever.

The *Lady* made only one combat mission; and her bombs were never dropped in anger. With twelve other

B-24's making up Section B of Mission number 109, the *Lady* took off at about 2 p.m., April 4, 1943, with orders to participate in high-altitude bombing at Naples. The target was some 750 miles distant from the *Lady's* airfield at Soluch, Libya; and owing to a howling sandstorm at takeoff half of the bombers developed engine trouble and aborted. None of the planes in Section B made it to Naples.

Only one of them didn't make it back to Soluch.

In the years since the *Lady's* ill-fated mission, records and discoveries have finally solved her mystery. The story reveals much about human greatness and human error; about the effect of bad communications and about the sometimes-tragic result of making assumptions unnecessarily when facts could be obtained in their place.

By 7:30 p.m. on the night of her mission, only four aircraft had come within 30 miles of Naples. Lieutenant W. J. Hatton, piloting the *lady Be Good,* assumed command and ordered everyone to turn back for Soluch. It was the last time the other three pilots ever heard his voice.

The *Lady* had flown some 700 miles riding a strong tailwind, and so both Hatton and Navigator-lieutenant Dp Hays made their first critical assumption: They would be bucking a headwind on the return flight. Circumstances began, a chain of events which would ultimately destroy them: The wind had shifted. It was not slowing them down; it was pushing them.

There were enemy aircraft in the April skies in 1943, and so the *Lady* and her sisters observed radio silence. It was something they were familiar with, something that had become a habit. Habits can be, sometimes, as deadly as assumptions: We may presume that because they were not using the other radio gear, the same habit impelled them to ignore their radio/automatic direction finder. The ADF was never turned on; even though this particular instrument is a receiver, not a transmitter, and could not have jeopardized radio silence.

Lieutenant L. A. Worley, the last B-24 from Section Two to return, touched down at Soluch at about 11:10 that night. At his debriefing, he mentioned that he had been following *Lady Be Good.* This piece of information might have saved most of the *Lady's* crew, but it went unnoticed for a dozen years amid the stacks of reports in the flight operations office at Soluch. A lack of communications joined the sequence of events, welding another link into the chain of circumstances that was being wrapped around the crew of the *Lady Be Good.*

Sixty-two minutes later, at 12:12 p.m., the tower adjacent to Soluch field received the last transmission from the *Lady.* Breaking silence because they were now close to base, the crew asked for an inbound radio direction finder fix on their course. The tower reported they were right on heading 330 degrees magnetic—precisely on course. Nobody was aware until years afterward that the *Lady* was more than an hour behind the B-24 which had been *following.*

Hatton's crew *couldn't* still be approaching Soluch; and they weren't. They had already passed the base, missing it completely because of their altitude and the obscured visibility. They thought they were still over the Mediterranean, because they were allowing for a headwind that wasn't there.

Had their ADF been turned on, the needle would have revolved through a complete circle as they flew over the tower. Everyone on board would have understood what that meant.

Had the tower operator known about Lieutenant Worley's remark that he was following the *Lady*, he would have known something was very, very wrong. Not knowing, he responded as he should have when asked for an approach bearing radio fix.

In 1943, radio direction finding equipment used a loop-shaped antenna which gave the strongest "reading" when an incoming signal was perpendicular to the loop. By rotating the antenna, the operator was able to determine that the *Lady* was on an inbound course, relative to the tower, of 330 degrees magnetic.

However, this R.D.F. equipment had one flaw: It was equally as sensitive from either the "front" or the "back" side of the loop. The *Lady* had passed over the tower, the R.D.F. was picking up her transmissions on the back side of the loop, and the tower operator had no way of knowing. Asked for an inbound heading fix, he gave it; he would have given a fix of 150 degrees, *with the same reading*, had Hatton asked for an outbound position check. The difference—180 degrees—was a matter of life or death.

The tower operator was already talking to dead men on a doomed aircraft...it was then only a question of time and steadily-draining fuel tanks.

As the fuel ran out, Hatton shut down the *Lady's* engines one at a time, feathering the props to reduce drag. They were still trying to reach Soluch...still fighting for distance against the headwind...when Hatton knew they were finished. Trimming the *Lady's* controls for level flight, with only one engine still running, he ordered the crew to get ready to bail out...

...into the water. They were, in reality, fast approaching the Egyptian/Lybian border, deep in the Sahara Desert.

One man's parachute didn't open. The others, landing in desert sand, finally realized what had happened. They began hiking toward Soluch, to the north, apparently believing the base was not far away.

Desert experts said no human being could walk more than 25 miles in this hellish place of 125 degree heat and merciless sun by day; freezing temperatures at night. Nor would a person live for more than two days; whether he walked or not, whether he had all the water he could carry...

The *Lady's* remaining crewmen had less than half a canteen of water among them. They walked, stopping to make arrowshaped markers with rocks and parachute remnants; to try to rest during the nights of agonizing cold. Five of them went on for eight days and nights, covering almost 70 miles, before they stopped for the last time. Three others—unbelievably—kept going:

They have never been found. They didn't do it with food and water and shelter...they did it with guts and faith and hope.

But it was futile. Even enduring more than twice the time and distance a human could be expected to survive, these poignantly courageous men had no chance.

They had obviously made one last assumption: The *Lady Be Good*, they apparently reasoned, had run out of fuel and plummeted into the Sahara, disintegrating. They began walking toward Soluch. On a heading 180 degrees from the direction they took, and less than a dozen miles away, the *Lady* was waiting for them. She's still there, today. She would probably have saved their lives.

The B-24 had continued after the crew bailed out. Slowly she lost altitude; her weight steadily overpowering the single remaining engine. When she finally ran out of fuel, the *Lady Be Good* gently pancaked into the sand, an almost-flawless belly-landing, and skidded to a stop.

Seventeen years later when the search team finally reached her...after the *Lady* was accidentally spotted by an oil-company geologist on a flight in search of oil...she was still almost unharmed.

There was drinkable coffee in a thermos on board. There were rations in abundance; virtually unaged in the timeless heat and dryness of the Sahara. Nothing was rusted. The radio equipment was still in operating condition.

Ultimately, six crewmen went home to rest in peace. Three will remain, perhaps, keeping silent company with the desert wind, forever. The *Lady* will wait for them, probably forever: There is no way to get her off that plateau, and no reason to. People will not bother her: To go there is suicide. Nothing ever rusts or rots in that weather. She remains, a touching monument to human courage; and to the sometimes-tragic results of circumstances, assumption, habit, emotion and 180-degree errors in the lives of ordinary people.

How many times, in your life, have you struggled

against opposition which didn't really exist, bucking an imaginary headwind...?

How many times, in your life, have you been operating with your intuition "switched off;" the emotional equivalent of your Automatic Direction Finding system ignored...?

How many times, in your life, has a minor mis-communication resulted in major problem...? "...my B-24 was following Hatton's..."

How many times, in your life, have you taken readings "off the back side of the loop," making 180-degree errors in judgement...? ("I should have done just the opposite...")

How many times, in your life, have you assumed that help was much closer, more readily obtainable, than it turned out to be...?

How many times, in your life, have you shown extraordinary courage and endurance; only to be defeated by circumstances simply overwhelming...? (...nobody could walk more than 25 miles in that inferno—those guys went *70 miles*—my God, how magnificent...)

How many times, in your life, have you turned your back on the one thing that could help you, resolutely marching exactly the opposite direction; perhaps never knowing that help was 180 degrees away...?

The little-known, tragic and almost eerie story of the *Lady Be Good* is true. Her crew's awesome courage and faith can make us proud to share in their humanity. And the *Lady's* story lends a chilling illustration of the effect, in our lives, of the very common human condition we often share:

"Sometimes, I don't know whether I'm coming or going."

For the ten crewmen of the *Lady Be Good* the 180 degrees between coming and going—reading off the back side of the loop—was fatal.

In our lives, such mistakes aren't necessarily fatal; but they can be damaging, painful, heartbreaking. We can't avoid all such mistakes, but to avoid them more often than not is the only course...the only heading...leading to mental self-sufficiency.

May the crew of B-24 No. 124301—the *Lady Be Good*—rest forever in peace. And, if their story has helped some of us to a deeper insight to the concepts about to unfold before us...if any of us find emotional maturity and peace of mind in part because of those men...

Then Mission 109, the *Lady's* only assignment, was not in vain.

Forward

All human conduct, for good or evil, is the result of individuals making choices. Decisions precede actions and actions produce results; some good, some bad. The only real difference these results produce in life is a simple question of magnitude: The degrees ranging from satisfaction to sheer ecstasy; or from displeasure to personal tragedy.

When we do things well we have the sense of well-being that says we are "on course." When we mis-cope, we have lost our bearings. Such errors in judgement are so commonplace our language contains numerous expressions to describe them: "I should have done just the opposite," or "I did that backwards," or "I don't know whether I'm coming or going."

It isn't an accident that our everyday language is full of sayings which colorfully describe thought and action as being one hundred eighty degrees off course: One Eight Zero degrees from *any* point on the compass is the exact reverse; it is "the opposite," it is "backwards."

The cumulative effect of these life-mistakes brings failure to some people, anxiety and depression to others; and nobody is exempt from the effects of backwards judgement.

Becoming mentally self-sufficient would, for each of us, vastly improve the quality of foresight. Hindsight may be clearer, less distorted, but unfortunately hindsight can only show us where we've been...not where we are going. We all know how to look backwards, but life is 180 degrees from there: It is still in front of us.

Understanding *why* we make navigational errors in our lives, and knowing what to do about it, can help anyone achieve mental self-sufficiency. Such knowledge is not a system...not exactly; nor is it a "method," although there is method in its application. Nor is it either science or art or religion.

It is, instead, a theory; one which provides enough insight to *why* we do what we do to enable, if necessary, a complete turn-around in life.

A complete turn-around, of course is 180 degrees.

And this, on the following pages, is the 180-Degree Theory.

Chapter One

"Where Do I Begin...?"

Success. Everybody wants it; very few ever learn to define it, and incredibly few ever achieve it. Efforts range from a vague, gut-level longing to hyperactive lifestyles filled with ulcers, battered ego and demolished personality. Those in search of some hidden wisdom have a library filled with books on self improvement; books begun in excitement and forgotten almost before they were completed.

These books will tell you how to put the screws to your neighbor—or how to live with him in peace, love and joy. You can discover how to get rich in real estate; how to make the opposite sex go bananas when you walk into the room. You can learn the secrets of nonverbal communication or else find out how to improve your verbal communication.

Money, sex, love and power—it's all "out there," say these authors. If you're not getting your fair share, there's something wrong with you; something you lack that the latest book can help you with.

First, however, according to such books, you have to be someone different from who and what you are now. You have to shed your poor, unattractive, pitiful self for a brand-new, glittering *somebody.*

Wrong!

Who and what you are—your personality—is more than just difficult to change. It's virtually impossible to make you over into someone else without risking grave psychological damage. In later chapters you'll learn how to "peg" yourself into one of four "arch-types" and one of four sub-types within your major category. Everybody fits into one of these convenient compartments, unless the individual is in an institution—or headed for one.

Think of your basic personality as if it were the home you live in; because in many very real ways, it is. You can remodel it, landscape it differently, increase or decrease its value. You can change it in highly visible and often lasting cosmetic "remodeling;" sometimes you can even make some fairly extensive "structural" changes. But you *can't* change the foundation, or rip out the structural framework, without great effort and risk.

With a building it's often easier to simply get rid of the old one and build a new one.

With a human being, of course, that's impossible. Still, far too many people become so convinced the old "structure" is no good that they take the first step: They tear it down, get rid of it. We call that suicide; and while it's the most spectacular way to destroy a self-structure, it may not be the most painful. Other destructive behavior abounds in our society. You may recognize yourself in some of these.

Continuing the analogy to a house: How many instances can you recall in which someone rented a basically-sound house to people who treated it carelessly? The renter (in this case, the "user") had nothing to lose; so he constantly took away from the value without putting anything back. In many such cases, he finally simply decamped—not bothering even to pay the back rent or attempting to clean up his mess and repair some of the damage he'd done.

Nobody can even guess how many of us, today, think of our self-structure as "basically sound" but of no significant value—so we "rent ourselves out" to users. People get away with doing things to us, taking things from us, without any concern for the mess or damage they're creating. In most such relationships, we place a ridiculously low value upon ourselves. Frequently, when the user is finished with us, we don't even complain that he didn't keep his end of the bargain.

How many men or women are there, today, who are locked into a relationship—whether married, going steady, or simply paired off—in which the other partner constantly says or implies he or she is dissatisfied with sexual performance? Of such mis-matches the vital question is almost never asked: "Who is *really* the victim?" Many sexually-healthy, even sensual people have been almost ruined by a partner's sex problems. Psych-doctors call this cute little trick "transferance," or "projection." What it means is that the person with the problem alleviates it by smearing it all over someone who didn't have a problem—at first.

Is your nose ugly? —Don't laugh! One of the co-author's dearest friends is an intelligent, truly-beautiful, dynamic divorcee in her early 40's. She has so much going for her that she has problems, sometimes, with envy and jealousy from her female acquaintances. For years now she has looked forward to the day when her youngest child graduates, so she can sell her house and move to a new location—after spending a big chunk of the real estate income for a nose job. The truth is that nobody ever "sees" her nose until she mentions it; and yet no single day in her life goes by that she doesn't personally suffer from her own self-concept.

How many of us can't live up to the reputation of our mother or father or brother or sister?

How many of us can't *live down* the reputation of another family member?

How many of us have failed miserably in life because we weren't "rich" at 30...or 40...or 50?

How many truly gifted musicians earn a living playing in a piano bar evenings and weekends?

How many superb writers gave up because their work never got published?

The list, of course, is endless. What it all boils down to is this: How many lives are unrewarding—desperate—even destroyed, not because of any *genuine* problem...but because of "feelings?"

I may not *be* ugly, but if I *feel* ugly I will most certainly try my conscious and unconscious best to live as if I were repulsive.

I may not *need* a new car, but if my feelings of want for that new car become "so strong I can taste it," I'll probably cheat, borrow, beg or maybe even steal to get it, won't I?

I may not be able to dominate a sales meeting, because my basic self-structure simply may not be socially-dominant, but the *fact* that I'm not a dominant type gets buried beneath psycho-tons of *feelings* that "there's something wrong with me."

The 180-Degree Theory is a means of identifying who and what and where we are; a way of orienting ourselves as to personality, character, ideals and goals. It is also a tool which enables us to separate the reality from our feelings in given situations. Over and over, as you read this book, you will see evidence of the 180-Degree Theory in action. In a much-too-simple form, we might express the theory as: "When in doubt, turn about." How does it work? An illustration:

"Oh, well...Marianne's a bit sloppy, she drinks too much and she's slept around a bit—but maybe she'll change. Besides, I'm not getting any younger and I'm not such a prize, myself. She says she really loves me and wants to get married...maybe I'd better go with my emotions. Somebody once said, 'if it feels good, do it...!"

Wrong! If there's any doubt, turn about, my friend.

How about this one: "I *know* ABC Corporation will give me a big raise and I'm reasonably sure the company is going to really grow. But I'm afraid to pull out of XYZ Company because I've got ten years senority and my feelings are that Old Crankshaw will blacklist me if I quit. Besides, maybe I'll get a raise this year; I haven't had one for five years..."

Or put it in reverse: "I know my future is secure at Dull Data Developers but, wow! That guy from Scintillating Systems is something else! He thinks that as soon as we get through the recession, the company will make a fortune. I keep feeling like I might miss a real opportunity if I don't take a temporary cut in pay and move to Balitmore..."

Does this sound familiar...? "I can't see anything wrong with that new house south of town. It went on the market at $32,000; then went to $28,000 and finally $26,000. The Realtor told me today that I could have it for $25,500—but I have to buy it *right now...*" (Whoops!)

Obviously, the 180-Degree Theory is more than a catch-phrase to "turn-about." As you continue you'll find out ways to remodel your self-structure; always without trying to change the foundation or framework that is uniquely "you." What we are after is a certain amount of beneficial behavior modification.

We won't try to change a quiet, methodical individual into an effervescent life-of-the-party type. First of all, we'd have to assume there's something basically wrong with being quiet and moderate; and that it's better to be bubbly and outgoing. Of course, the reverse is true: If you tried to make a dynamic personality into a plodder it would be like trying to cap an artesian well—it won't work.

Many of the self-help ideas floating around these days all begin with the basic premise that *there's something wrong with what you are.* The 180-Degree Theory reverses that: There's not only nothing wrong with your basic self-structure (unless you need clinical help); *it's dangerous to try to change it!*

Another very popular theme is to rely on emotions, hunches, "feelings." "If it feels good..." The 180-Degree Theory will help you learn to identify the difference between *intuition* (which can be beneficial) and "feelings"—which, of course, are usually wrong more often than they're right.

Notice we're using averages, here: We're trying to be effective more often than not. If we can take two or three steps forward and only one backward, we're gaining. Run like the dickens from *any* concept or "ism" that promises to make you *always* effective. Horse manure! *Nobody* bats 1,000 in this game called life. At 500, you're breaking even. At 750, you're a winner. What we want is to create a way of living—the good, old "modus vivendi"—that consistently allows us to break the 500 barrier.

The 180-Degree Theory *works*. Dr. Nara has helped scores of people in a one-on-one basis. The theory helped Dr. Bob build an emotionally, financially and socially successful life. It helped Steve Mariner come from a 39-year-old failure, with his thumb on the "destruct" button, to a happy and well-adjusted life; able to do what he likes best—for money—achieving a measure of personal success he never dreamed of.

Moreover, the 180-Degree Theory is solidly based in well-researched psychological principles. Some more recent breakthroughs in clinical psychology tend to make the theory even stronger. Many earlier self-help "schemes" are wound around the writings of a scientist named Freud, whose own life and death left a great deal to be desired. Not enough attention, until recently, has been paid to the work of Dr. Karl Jung. Without delving into details, the shifting emphasis of the influence of these two alone is making major changes in the outlook of up-to-date counselors.

Dr. Nara's earlier book, *Feelings—Having An Encounter With Yourself,* was made available on a limited basis in 1976. Hundreds of people used that book to effect profound changes in their lives. These people, universally, have insisted that Dr. Bob expand the basic ideas of that earlier book and make the 180-Degree Theory available to everyone.

We want *you* to get off the merry-go-round of books that tell you you're no good. Instead, we offer a way for you to achieve a valid perspective of yourself and to use that basic structure to build your own successful life.

We don't want you to try to become something you can't be. Let's apply the 180-Degree Theory:

We want you to *become all you can be.*

We aren't going to hack away to find out what's bad about you, and then destroy it. Instead, we'll discover what is good about you, and reinforce it.

Will the 180-Degree Theory bring you money, sex, power and charm? —Is that really what you want? The 180-Degree Theory can't bring you *anything*; but it can help you achieve success. When you've completed the book, if you still equate success to money, sex, power and charm —why not? *Somebody* should have these things, right? Just be sure you know what you truly consider success—because you'll probably get it.

Chapter Two

"What Makes Me Tick?"

What is the real essence of a human being? All of us remember learning somewhere in our schooling that the human body is composed of chemicals and water, and that the value (even with runaway inflation) is ridiculously low. When a person dies very little changes immediately. In fact, the hair and fingernails still grow for a while.

The "engine" which drives us stops running when we die: Matabolism comes to a halt; the slow chemical reactions which cause us to be, usually, about 98.6 degrees warm internally. The heart stops pumping, blood stops moving. But we are still the same mass of chemicals and water! So—what did we "lose?"

What happens when a person dies is that the computers stop running and the data banks are "wiped." Before the religious or spiritual reader gets angry at that word, "computers," let's add that the human computers are like nothing mankind has ever designed.

Whether we call our mind-energy "brain waves" or "kinetic impulses" or "soul" or "spirit" we are still talking about the same thing. There is a brain-energy, very similar to electricity, which operates our mind and its related nerve network circuitry.

How does it work? —Who knows? Oh, science keeps finding clues, and the human mind is no longer a simple mystery. Now it's a very complicated mystery.

Why does it work? Now we are into a realm where

the spiritual, the religious, come into the fore. You could make a pretty good case against the necessity for a mind as capable as ours. As far as we know, no other critter on the face of the earth has anything even near as efficient.

In terms of sheer survival of the species, our mind is "overkill" to a ridiculous degree. We have a much lower survival index than a shark or a cockroach, when you come right down to it; neither of those creatures seems uncomfortable because it can't out-think a human being.

Many of us believe there is an inherent logic in the concept of a "creator," a universal force which endowed mankind with intelligence and "soul" for a reason. Huge numbers of us call this force "God," and there's no reason to fight with that. For those who personally are uncomfortable with that approach, it might be just as easy to add a letter, "o", and call it "Good."

The other side of the spiritual coin, of course, is known to many as "Devil." Again, to provide a word which is more acceptable to some folks, let's take away one letter, "d", and label this counter-force "evil."

Animals other than humans don't have any trouble with these concepts. Human beings have to deal with them all of their lives. To a dog, for example, the idea of good or bad, right or wrong simply doesn't exist. He can learn that some actions produce desirable results and others bring punishment: The nearest he ever gets to "right" and "wrong" is a sort of pain/pleasure understanding of his relationship with the world around him.

Only humans are blessed (or cursed) with the facility of mind which lets us ask ourselves, "I wonder if it would be *right* for me to do so-and-so...?" Or, as is so often the case, to be able to consider an action we really want to take, in the light of what it might do to another, and say, "I guess I'd better not do that...but, gee—I wish I could have."

Even before we get into a deeper discussion of how the mind works for or against us, it's time for the first of a number of *principles* this book will offer. Whenever and wherever you see one of these principles, study it very carefully, please. The authors consider these key points to be so vital that no life, in our opinion, will result in success if they are violated with any frequency. Living by these principles won't guarantee success; but failing to use them as life-guides will almost always guarantee failure.

Cheaters Never Win!

There seems to be a universal "law" in operation, something that is certainly not new to religious people, which tells us that evil brings evil. Make up your mind that for the rest of your life, you will never ignore the extremely dangerous pitfall of succumbing to the temptation to do something you *know* is *wrong*; so as to obtain some personal gain at another's expense.

The cheater, the user, the person who feeds on another's misfortune; the person who lies and steals (no matter how much you change the word "steal" into something more palatable), will almost certainly pay a terrible price sooner or later.

This book will provide many, many ways in which you can change your life to a more success-oriented, fulfilling style. There are many, many ways to "get ahead" in the world without climbing over someone else's rights to get there. We want you to begin thinking in terms of being involved only in "win-win" situations. The only lasting "deals" in life are those in which everybody wins. Try to avoid situations where there will be a "winner" and a "loser" —even if you are the winner, and especially if you are the loser.

Now let's take a look at the mind—not a scientific examination of its mechanics, but a practical view of what it does.

We're going to continue using the analogy of computers, because it makes a lot of sense and helps us understand "what makes us tick." For example, the mind has one section which deals only with engineering and housekeeping. This computer runs without any conscious effort on our parts whatsoever: It is the "system" that tells the heart to pump, the lungs to inhale and exhale, the ears to hear, the eyes to see, nerve endings to feel.

Picture, if you will, a huge computer complex. In one section, perhaps labeled "plant management," there would be ranks and ranks of machines with prerecorded memories. With no supervision whatsoever, these computers function 24 hours a day for a lifetime. If they didn't, we'd be dead—right now! Can you imagine how terrifying simply going to sleep would be if there was the slightest hint that our "heartbeat computer" couldn't run without supervision...or if it was planning to go on strike at midnight?

Another room—a vast room, longer than the eyes can see—would be labeled "cognition section." That's your "thinker." Another department would be called "conative section." That's your "feeler"—the source of emotion.

Now, obviously these computers are all inter-connected. The main computer—the cognitive computer—is the "boss." It tells the others what to do; and it gets "input" from them which it uses to make decisions... about us.

How many times have you said, either aloud or to yourself, "I can't do that!" when someone suggests a course of action. You didn't stop and think it through, carefully, before you responded: You *reacted.* Essentially, the super-computer "rang down" to the sub-computer and said: "Such-and-such has been proposed. Look in the memory banks and see if we have that capability." The sub-computer ran through the data and replied, "no way!" Result: "I can't do that."

Maybe that was true; and *maybe it wasn't.* Why? Well, to put it fairly bluntly, the sub-computer can lie to the super-computer, and *it frequently does.* The reverse is true, too: Your super-computer "programs" your sub-computer all the time, day in and day out.

Supposing you think of yourself as un-athletic, awkward and timid; and you think of yourself in this not-necessarily-true manner whenever you consider physical activity.

What kind of information will your sub-computer find in its data bank when you're invited to go downhill skiing? You got that right: "I can't do that!"

Why says you *really* can't? Did you ever try?

When we've finished showing you how to manage your twin computers more successfully, the situation would be very different. Invited to go skiing, your conscious mind would be given a completely different reaction: "I wonder how well I could do, if I tried?" Why? When the "order" went in for a memory-bank search, the subconscious would answer, "insufficient data," meaning that your *conscious* mind will have to handle the situation.

You'll trade a "feeling" of incompetence for the right to *decide*, with your "thinker," whether you want to give it a go or not.

What we want to do, simply stated, is show you how to make your sub-computer, your subconscious, quit lying to your thinking mind...and reserve the right for your conscious mind to lie to the subconscious any time it wants to—and, before we're done, it will want to do just that; quite often.

We've used two words, "cognitive" and "conative." Let's study them, because understanding these two concepts is *basic* to the 180-Degree Theory.

The cognitive ability of a human mind is what makes us (or breaks us) as individuals. We're familiar with the statement of a philosopher named Descartes: "Cogito, ergo sum;" "I think; therefore I am." One dictionary describes cognition as:

Cognition (n): Action or faculty of *knowing, perceiving, conceiving, as opposed to emotion and volition;* a perception, sensation, notion, or intuition.

No matter how you turn that definition about, looking at it, it always comes out the same: Cognition means *to know*. And it means knowledge as distinctly *separate* from both emotion (feelings) and voltion (involuntary reactions).

For our purposes, there are two "kinds" of "knowing:" There is the knowing that comes from reasoning, using all the facts at hand, and coming up with deductions that make sense; and there is the intuitive knowledge: Those rare cases when you are *absolutely sure* about something without really understanding how you "got that way."

Now let's take a look at *conative* processes, which the same dictionary gives very short shrift indeed:

Conation (n): Desire to perform an action, volition, voluntary action; hence, 'conative.'"

Did you see anything in there about "thinking?" —No, and you won't, either. Conative information rattling around in our heads is *feelings* when we are aware of it, and it is the involuntary "housekeeping" of a heart that pumps, lungs that breath, etc.

There's a place for conative processes in our lives, of course. We'd be dead without them, for one thing; and life (while it lasted) would be worthless and sterile. Conative processes are responsible for the delicious "feelings" we have when we are in love. They reward us by giving us feelings when we smell a dew-laden rose.

And the conative network does more than simply reward us and keep our physical plant operating. If you heard a loud buzzing noise immediately behind you as you read this, you'd react so as to avoid a bee-sting. If you had to go through a cognitive, thinking process before your avoidance mechanism went into action, you'd get stung more likely than not.

The problem so many of us face throughout life is that our conative, our subconscious, gets too big for its britches. It tries to do our thinking for us, and it will to a very big extent if we let it. It makes sense, when you think about it. The conscious mind relies completely on the subsconscious for so much information that the "input" is constantly open. The conscious allows the subconscious to "over-ride" any time it has to for our safety; as in the bee-sting example above.

Now, obviously, because the interconnect design of these computers intentionally permits a good deal of guidance by the subconscious, the "circuits" are always open. As a result, *all of us allow the subconscious to make decisions it has no right to make*—from sheer force of habit.

"I can't ski."

"That good-looking secretary in receiving would never look twice at me."

"The bank would never loan me the money for that new car."

"The fish won't bite today."

"I can whip that big bully with one hand behind me."

Are any of the above true? Any of them *may* be true, but the subconscious has no way of *knowing*—unless the conscious mind has carefully analyzed all of the data and made a thoughtful decision...or unless we've actually tried and found out through experience that something is true or false.

Until we arrive at a *cognitive* decision about life, any input from our *conative* mind-center is a *feeling*; and experience has shown us that feelings are wrong so often we'd be way ahead of the game if we *always did just the opposite.*

Why do you suppose General George Armstrong Custer pulled a bone-head stunt that got him and all of his men killed, at the famous "Custer's Last Stand?" Only a horse survived this debacle. Now, Custer was not new to combat. You don't get to be a general because your shoes shine better than the other men's. He *knew* how to "fight injuns."

You can almost "feel", as you think about it, what Gen. Custer was "feeling" that day. The Business Publication Audit of Circulation, Inc., uses Gen. Custer's unfortunate last stand in an advertisement illustrating the importance of accurate numbers. It's such a good "memory-peg" that we are going to use it here:

> On June 25, 1876, George Armstrong Custer ignored his scouts' warnings of many Indians gathered at Little Big Horn. So he rode out with 250 men to "surround" 6,000 Indians. This was a serious error.

The point? —What destroyed 251 men that day at Little Big Horn...cognitive reasoning, or conative reacting? Did Gen. Custer use his "head" or his "feelings" that day? What if Gen. Custer had thoroughly understood and used the 180-Degree Theory?

Remember what Descartes said, "I *think*; therefore I am?" Custer showed us the other side of the coin: "I *feel*, therefore I'm dead!"

Feelings have an extremely worthwhile place in our lives; if we can learn not to "think" with them. Feelings are for enjoyment—even for sorrow; because life wouldn't be real if we couldn't react to the loss of a loved one, for instance. Feelings are the icing on the cake of life; and everyone should learn to enjoy them to the utmost. But don't *think* with your *feeler*. That's backwards! Or, as in the little story above, "this is a serious error."

How long has this been going on? Well, would you believe St. Paul the apostle? In his letter to the Romans, he said:

> So I find it to be a law that when I want to do right, evil lies close at hand. For I delight in the law of God, in my inmost self, but I see in my members another law *at war with the law of my mind* and making me captive...

Begin thinking of the relationship between your conscious and unconscious mind(s) as a benign state of war: The subconscious mind is going to keep trying to govern your actions by *feelings*; you'll have to constantly program your conscious mind to be on the alert for this. Remember always that your subconscious is a *servo-mechanism:* It is there to serve your conscious mind and your physical "plant." The subconscious is, for all its great ability, little more than an idiot when it comes to making decisions.

Those of us who don't care to have our life run by an idiot have to take steps to prevent our subconscious from having any say in final decisions. Think of this sort of dialog between the conscious and the subconscious:

"Hey, stupid: I have to make a decision about which car to buy. How do you feel about it?"

"Well, I sure like the red one. It's pretty!"

"Is that all you have to say? Well, the red one is about double what our budget can handle. Besides, it's a gas-hog."

"I don't care!", the subconscious insists, "I want the red one. I *want* it!"

"You said that already," the conscious replies. "But, all things considered, we're going to buy the blue one."

"No!" screams "feelings," "Buy the red one. The red one!"

"Shut up, stupid," the conscious orders...and the subconscious (once you get the hang of it) will mind the boss.

Because the subconscious is dependent on the conscious, it has one curious property...and one that we are going to put to good use. It will believe anything the conscious mind tells it. *Anything!* Because it is a slave-computer without *any* reasoning ability, it accepts whatever programming we want to put into it. This can be carried to unusual extremes, for example, in mind-control techniques such as Yoga: The subconscious can even be re-programmed so that the automatic "plant maintenance" systems are under direct command of the thinking mind. In such situations, as you know, a practitioner of these arts can raise or lower his body temperature; can change the rate of heartbeat and respiration, can even make his nerves insensitive to intense heat or other pain stimuli.

We don't suggest that it's necessary to go to such lengths. However, the existence of such techniques proves that the cognitive mind can control the conative mind to nearly unbelievable extent. Whatever we "tell" our subconscious, it accepts as absolute truth.

We do this all the time; usually to our detriment. We can become virtually enslaved by feelings that have no relationship whatsoever to reality.

Years ago, the co-author developed a sebaceous cyst on his left cheek. This lump grew to rather large size, giving his face two profiles: One for his nose, the other for his "lump." Although he was almost always aware of it; and was sure people stared at it, he did nothing about having it removed.

Why? It didn't make any difference, you see, because *he was ugly anyway.* How did he *know* he was ugly? Well, when he was 14 or 15 he already had a heavy enough beard that he had to shave every morning before going to school. In the harsh, merciless glare of the bathroom light, every day, he stared into a gawky-looking face riddled with acne; at a head of unruly hair that did *nothing* he wanted it to do.

He spent about 15 minutes *every day* telling his subconscious that he was *ugly*; that nobody could feel anything but revulsion.

And so, in his mid-30's, a cyst came along which really *did* make him ugly. And he did nothing about it, because of *feelings* that he was ugly, anyway—so why bother? In fact, the cyst *reinforced* lifetime feelings; it *proved them right.*

Fortunately he had to visit a doctor for something completely unrelated to the cyst, and while in the office, the doctor said, "Let's get rid of that lump while you're here; it looks like hell."

How many of us argue with doctors? —The lump went. And years later, through the benefit of the 180-Degree Theory, so did the feelings of ugliness.

Today, it makes no difference whether Steve

Mariner is "handsome" or "ugly" —he's neither, actually—but he has learned how to program his subconscious with an acceptable self-image. He has no "feelings" about his appearance, one way or the other. And why should he? No amount of *feelings* will amend his physical appearance...nor will it *yours*. What we look like is a *fact*; and we can learn to accept it, find out how to present it in its most flattering light, and live with it.

Remember in chapter one the example of a beautiful woman who suffers emotionally because she thinks her nose is ugly? Why does she feel that way, if it isn't true? It's *because the subconscious will believe anything we tell it...*whether it's true or not.

That is one of the most basic "tools" we have to work with, and we will use it over and over again. We are going to develop the habit of lying to our subconscious whenever we wish, and using it to better ourselves. This principle will be covered in chapter nine, under the heading, "Acting your way to a new feeling."

For the remainder of this book, then, we need to think of our "selves," our minds, as having three basic "departments." These are the physical plant maintenance department, the emotion-factory, and the thinker.

The plant maintenance department will operate without any input from us, so we'll virtually ignore it. It's there to serve us; and it will, so we simply let it do its thing.

The emotion-factory, the feelings fabrication center, the conative part of the mind, we are going to put on a short leash: This section of our mind is going to learn, once and for all, who is "boss" in our lives.

The cognitive part of our mind, the part that makes us what we are, the part that is the "I" in our lives, is going to finally come into its own: We are going to learn how to be all that we can be, free at last from hang-ups and mis-direction from our emotions. We're going to learn how to avoid "serious errors" like General Custer made; as well as how to live life more abundantly, more rewardingly. We begin by asking a question: "*Who do you think you are...?*"

Chapter Three

'Who Do You Think You Are?'

If we asked you to describe yourself—not your physical appearance, but your personality—as best you could, and then took that description to your closest acquaintances, do you think they could guess who we were talking about?

If you guessed "yes," you'll be surprised to learn that very few people can describe themselves accurately enough so that someone else could identify them from that description. The reasons for this are legion, but it's a good bet that one of the most significant is that we describe a hybrid when we think of ourselves: We talk about some of our real attributes—and we add a good many characteristics we'd *like* to have, and don't.

If, for example, I think the late, great John Wayne would be an ideal to pattern my own personality after; if I want that very much to be part of me, I'll include it in my self description in one of two ways:

—I'll add a liberal seasoning of Wayneishness to myself, whether it's visible to others or not...

—Or I'll describe myself as just the opposite (because I'm not sure how well I've copied Mr. Wayne). Incidentally, if I go the latter way, I'll exclude those traits from my own inventory, again, whether they are visible or invisible to others.

By the way: If I *did* want to imitate John Wayne's personality, the odds are three to one against my coming anywhere near to it, and something like fifteen to one that I'll never come near enough for another person to recognize it. In fact, I'll probably damage myself emotionally trying to become something I'm not, and then add another failure to my growing list of life-failures.

To make matters absolutely dismal, I'll have to "live with" the knowledge that the turkey across the hall, that dumb so-and-so who still owes me five bucks, acts like John Wayne *all the time*—without, apparently, even trying.

That's right: He isn't trying; and it isn't an act. He happens to have the same personality type and sub-type as Mr. Wayne. As far as we can determine, about one in sixteen people will be like that "accidentally." It has nothing to do with trying to "be"—we are what we are and, barring a mind and soul-searing trauma, a true life-changing episode, we are (now) what we are going to remain as long as we live.

About half of us are going to be effervescent, expressive folks who make sweeping gestures, who love the "floor" at a meeting or party. These are the scintillating (sometimes overbearing) conversationalists; these are the people who embrace others in public, do a lot of back-slapping and in general seem very comfortable when they are "expressing themselves."

The other half of us tend to use fewer gestures and/or use "abortive" gestures. Instead of a full-arm sweep to point out a direction, we're more likely to keep our hand closer to the body and point with a finger. Often times a person such as this will sit for a long while at a meeting or a party, virtually motionless, listening to others and not saying anything.

In other words, this aspect of personality ranges from loose and free-wheeling at one end of the scale to very secretive and self-contained at the other.

The other "personality" dimension, aside from expressiveness or lack of it, is the "declare/inquire" index. Some of us will tend to be more assertive: "I'll *tell* you what I think...!", or "Here, let me show you a better way to do that..." The others will use a question, instead; or perhaps they'll preface a statement with a small disclaimer that (to them) takes the "hook" off it.

"I may be wrong," such a person will say, "But unless you already know it won't work, there may be a different way to do that..."; or "Do you mind if I give you my opinion about that?"

If you could rate yourself (or another) on a scale of one to ten on the index of indrawn to outgoing, and think of that as a horizontal line, it would look something like this:

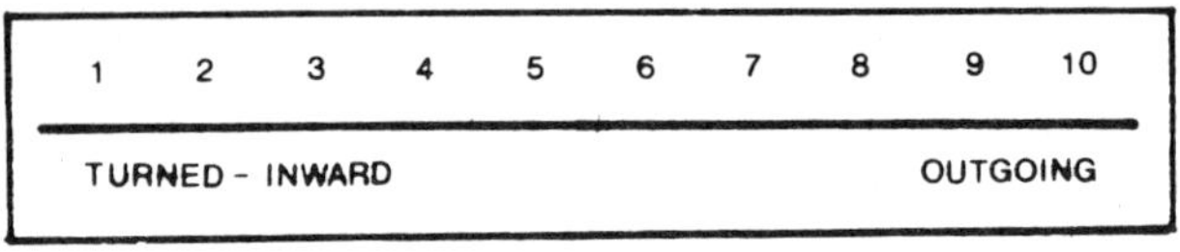

Then supposing you rated yourself, or someone else, on a scale of one to ten on the declare/inquire index, this time using a vertical scale intersecting the other, like this:

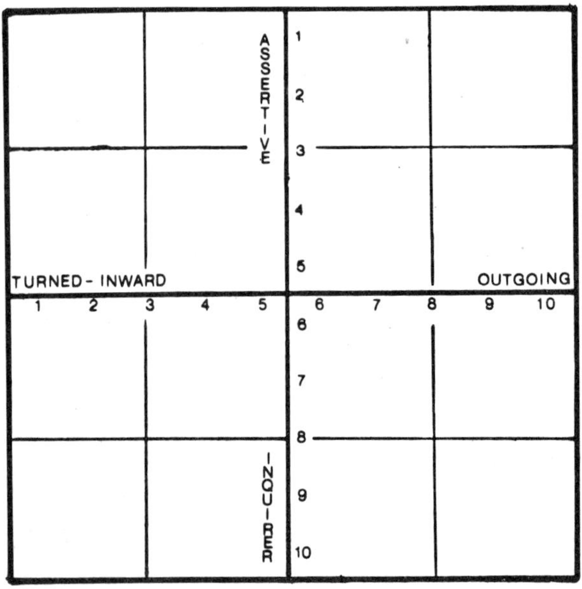

Of course, you noticed that we "cheated" by adding more lines, so that instead of four squares or quadrants, there are sixteen. Now—what do these little boxes mean?

Let's look at the four basic personality classifications, one at a time, to see how our "boxes" fit them...or, rather, how such people fit the boxes.

First: Think of someone you know who is very secretive; a person who seldom uses many gestures and, when he does, such gestures are often rather vestigial: What would have been a full-blown shoulder shrug in others will be a barely-seen lift of the shoulder in this person. (Incidentally, we used the word "he" —these traits have no sex and apply equally to male or female. Now and then in this book we will use "he" when the phrase "he and/or she" is cumbersome and will not genuinely help the reader to understand a shade of meaning.)

At any rate, we've begun picturing somebody: A person of few gestures; very economically done. This person will be "reserved," but *not necessarily shy.* In fact, he may be quite "pushy" when he wants his way. He is reserved in the sense that he isn't given to "bubbling" —he isn't very expressive.

Once again, be careful with words: When we say this person is not expressive, that does not mean he or she isn't articulate—capable of precise communication. Perhaps, to help with this, we should employ an almost-redundant phrase and say that this person will not be expansively expressive.

Since we are "designing" a human being, let's say that these traits are very evident. We'd think of this individual as "wooden," or "a stick." He's so deadpan, so much of the time, that we can safely rate him as a "1" on the 1 to 10 scale: He's totally "turned-inward."

Now let's think about whether this person is "bossy" or "mellow" —does he preface suggestions with a smooth way of making it seem that he isn't trying to dominate; or does he usually say something like,

"Listen, I'll tell you what I think you should do..."?

For our construction, we'll say that he's a definite "pusher." He'll watch for less than ten seconds as you fumble with a hammer and nail, then he'll reach for them with a curt, "Here—Give me that damn thing!" —And then *he* drives the nail...not necessarily better than you would have, but *his* way. He might even "justify" his action by telling you bluntly that if you don't know what you're doing, you shouldn't be trying to do it.

Got the picture? Okay: This person is a definite "1" on the assertive—inquirer scale. On our chart, that puts him all the way to the left (turned-inward "1") and all the way to the top (assertive—inquirer "1")

Now that we've got this individual "pegged," let's label him. He is a "pusher." Not everybody will be a clear-cut 1/1 on the scale, but these traits will be evident enough to establish that the person is *more* assertive than mellow; *more* reserved than expansive. Anyone tending toward the top and left of the graph is a "pusher," and the more obvious the characteristics are, the more that person is a classic example of this personality type.

Let's take our next case: This time, to be fair, we'll pretend we're describing a woman. She, like the pusher, is reserved, indrawn, not given to much expressiveness; she seldom gestures and is considered "quiet" in her circle of acquaintances. Let's give her a "1" on the turned-inward scale.

However, she differs greatly from the pusher in that she wouldn't be caught dead "telling" someone something. She never says, "Let me tell you how *I* do that..." She's the old smoothie that will suggest, or make her point with an innocent question: "I wonder if that bolt would come off easier if you turned it the other way...?" Now, she *knows* the lug nuts on her car are reverse-threaded, and she is *sure* you can turn them counter-clockwise until you're blue in the face, only making them tighter. But, instead of saying, "I know what's wrong: You have to turn them to the right," she'll say, "I wonder..." —or perhaps, she might ask, "Do you mind if I make a suggestion...?"

So she's a "1" —all the way to the left; and she's a "10"; all the way to the bottom. She is an "examiner." You will learn, shortly, why we've given her that label. For now: Everyone who clearly demonstrates characteristics of being reserved and quiet; and who usually avoids being "pushy" or assertive or dominant, is an examiner type.

Our third person is also a "10" on the assertiveness scale, clear at the bottom of the chart. He has the same way of taking the "sting" out of suggestions as the clever lady above. In fact, such people are not above making up a little white lie to get their points across without seeming overbearing. This gent, for example, if he found you trying to turn reverse-threaded lugs the wrong way, might say something like: "You know, I saw a service station attendant fixing a tire on a Belchfire 8 car like yours the other day; and he worked for ten minutes with an air-wrench before he tried turning them backwards..."

Of course, there was no such episode: This person, the "10—unassertive," will offer an imaginary scapegoat when he tells you you're a dummy: *He* doesn't want to take the "blame" for *telling* you something. If he can't get his point across by innocent question or mild suggestion, he'll "tell you a story."

However, this person also gives us our first glance at someone on the right-hand side of the chart: While he shares the full-scale "10" at the bottom, with the "examiner type" lady, he is the first we've seen of the very expressive sort. Now we see someone making gestures; and not just little ones, either: Full arm sweeps, huge shoulder shrugs. The face will never be at rest as this guy smiles, "makes faces," winks at people.

If *he* was the one telling that little fib about the gas station attendant changing an imaginary tire, his hands and arms would be going a mile-a-minute while he "showed you" how the mechanic handled the air-wrench; and his face would contort as he imitated the expressions of the hapless repairman. He'd probably even "grunt" as he tried to turn the make-believe lug nut the wrong way.

Can you see him, excited and waving his arms about, as he squats down next to you and bubbles, "Hey, Harry...do you mind if I make a suggestion? I mean, maybe I'm full of you-know-what, but what if this car has backwards threads on the lugs, you know...?"

The hallmark of such as this type is sensitivity toward others—toward relationships. For this reason, we call him or her a "sensitive." This individual goes to great lengths to be a pacemaker; he or she is usually inordinately concerned about what other people feel or think.

Last but by no means least is the person at the top right of the scale. We've saved this for last because this individual doesn't need us to be concerned about "his place." He'll take care of that, himself.

He is *assertive*; he's a "teller" not an asker. And he is so expressive as to be flambouyant much of the time. To him, the whole world's a stage, and he wants front center—all the time. If he overheard an argument in an elevator, he'd be exercising real self control not to interrupt and interfere, giving the contestants the benefit of his opinion...even if the others were total strangers; and he only heard the middle of an all-day haggle.

We'll label this type "outspoken," because that is one of the hallmark attributes of the clan. This is the effervescent person, the life of the party; the loud voice in the meeting room and the booming laughter rolling across the salesroom floor.

Let's recap the types before we move on to what these different folks are all about:

THE PUSHER—Look for assertiveness; for declaratory rather than inquiring statements; "I'll *tell* you" approaches. The other give-away is the tendency to be indrawn, showing a true economy of gestures, expressions, voice inflections. This person will be assertive, often overbearing; and will not show much outwardly, is a "poker face."

THE EXAMINER—As economical with expressions as the pusher, this person is totally different in that he or she seldom uses declaratory statements. Think of a poker face and few gestures; along with a tendency to ask rather than tell: "Would you mind if I made a suggestion...?"

THE SENSITIVE—Also an "asker," rather than a pushy type. Similar to the "examiner" in this respect, but totally different in outward expressions. This person gestures fluently; uses voice inflections to emphasize points. He or she is very outgoing. Generally, this person would fit the description, "mellow."

THE OUTSPOKEN—A flambouyant individual, this person is the most expressive of the lot. He or she is socially uninhibited and will tend to gravitate toward the center of the action. He or she is assertive to a large degree, and the sort who seems almost compelled to deliver an opinion on any subject at hand, and to identify his opinion with himself: "I'll tell you what I think," or "In *my* opinion..."

Who Is The Pusher?

Because of his assertiveness together with his tendency to avoid expressive display, this person is often misunderstood as a human being. To many, he or she will be aloof and self-contained; sure of where he is and where he's going.

The truth is that the pusher shares with all of us an "emotion factory," the feelings served up all the time by the subconscious. He or she can be deeply hurt in an interpersonal situation—but would bleed to death on the inside before any of it showed on the outside.

This is the person you work with, or deal with at some point in your life (maybe your neighbor), about whom you've more or less concluded you don't particularly like him...but that it probably doesn't matter to him whether you do or not.

If you are a pusher you probably feel a vague pang of doubt from time to time, something like, "I wonder why people seem to be cool toward me sometimes...? What do I do that makes them act like they don't want me around...?"

If you are more of a classic pusher rather than just having these dominant tendencies, you will follow up such half-formed "wonderings" with a terse self-instruction: "To hell with them—I haven't got time to go through life worrying about people's feelings!"

Time is far more important to a pusher than to others. It's a curious thing, but very true: The pusher is always aware of how much time is being devoted to any activity, or how much time will have to be invested in deciding a course of action. He or she is considered impatient by close associates.

If a salesman told a pusher who owned a firm, or was a purchasing agent, that there was a system on the market, new, that would absolutely double the firm's income—guaranteed—the pusher's next question (while glancing at his watch) would be, "How long will it take to tell me about it?"

The reader who is a pusher will find nothing unusual in that last paragraph...it makes sense to him. Those of us who are *examiners* or *sensitives* probably nodded as we read it, because we know people like that—and they're all nuts, right? The *outspoken* probably agrees with the pusher about the time, but he'd already be trying to figure out how to steal the salesman's thunder and wondering why he didn't think of the new idea first.

If a salesman guaranteed to double your income, *what does it matter how long it takes him to tell you about it?* —But for the pushers of the world, and to a certain extent the outspokens, this idea of time will always be important. If you want to drive a pusher or an outspoken right up the wall; if you want to see how to get him or her truly uncomfortable, just find a way to dawdle and waste his or her time.

Is a pusher's time more important, really, than an examiner's or a sensitive's? Not really: We are all allocated precisely 24 hours a day and what we do with it is our business—or our perogative—so its importance is something for personal evaluation.

To a pusher, it's important. Always.

The pusher is goal-oriented; he or she will always try to "get on with it" when there is a job to be done. "C'mon, c'mon—let's go!" Here again, those who are not pushers will think of this as a tendency toward impatience. How you go about doing something is, to a pusher, of little importance; the important thing is *doing* it.

Think of trying to drive a three-inch nail into the side of a building. Now, there's a one-inch siding board on that wall and behind it is a steel framework. You'll do fine until the nail is 1/64th of an inch beyond the wood and then—full stop; bent nail. The nail-driver *doesn't know* what's behind the wood. Got the picture?

The pusher will react almost predictably: He'll either go for a bigger hammer or swing harder with the one he's using. About the time the second or third nail hits bottom and bends, he'll begin to get impatient. If he has a colorful vocabulary, he'll start to color the area blue with invective against the nail, the hammer and the board.

When he finally faces the fact that the nail won't go into the wood more than an inch, he is very likely to "get mad", throw the hammer down and stalk off. He is job-oriented, goal-inspired. He came there to drive a nail; he tried his best, and it didn't work. To hell with it: You can't *put* a nail in that board! (If *he* couldn't, nobody can.)

People with other personality types, especially the sensitives but most especially the examiners, would not react in this manner. They'd wonder why the pusher acted like he did, and probably conclude that he or she is childish and prone to temper tantrums.

Others would ask themselves, the *first* time the nail suddenly bent double, "I wonder what caused that...?"

Not the pusher. He'd mutter, "That SOB..." and reach for another nail.

It's this goal-orientation that makes pushers rather insensitive to other people's feelings. That *does not* mean the pusher has no feelings: We all do. But, you see, if your basic personality type *drives* you to get on with it, to get the job done, you don't spend any time wondering about how others feel or what they think.

If a human being "bends" while a pusher is trying to do something, the pusher will treat that situation just like the nail: He'll swing harder, or get a bigger hammer. If someone else is getting in his way, he will run right over them if he has to, because to him the goal is important.

Does he think "the end justifies the means?" Not this person. He or she *isn't interested* in the means... *only* the end.

If you frustrate a pusher enough his emotions will override his thinking. This is true of everybody, not just the pushers, and it's important to remember: When someone is faced with a situation which puts them into personality discomfort, *the emotion factory goes into automatic over-ride.*

When that happens to a pusher, his first line of defense; his automatic reaction to get back to his "comfort zone," is to become dictatorial. This initial reaction is what gives him or her the name "pusher," because when it happens, these folks get "pushy" in a highly-visible manner.

This is the "bigger hammer" the pusher goes for: He or she will start issuing orders and making demands in a highly autocratic manner. From there on, it's all downhill...

If the pusher is the boss he or she can "get away" with this dictator method of relieving personality discomfort. The fact that others are forced to accede to the demands—or have their jobs threatened—makes it easy for the pusher-boss to use this escape method.

If he or she *isn't* the boss, the pusher's demanding ways often work almost as well, because other personality types (as we'll see later) are prone to permit this behavoir on the part of pushers (and outspokens).

But...what is the cost, to the pusher, of taking this emotion-laden escape route from personal discomfort? True, the tirade, the orders and threats probably got the desired results: Everybody "got on with" the job at hand, and that made the pusher comfortable again.

Employees would think, even as they followed orders, "He doesn't have to talk to me like that. What's the matter with him, anyway? Doesn't he think I know *anything?* What was *wrong* with doing it my way?" After enough of these episodes, the employees learn to do what they're told, when they're told to do it—and whether they like it or not.

What happens to fresh thinking, new ideas, progress and initiative in such a relationship? —Right: They go away.

What happens to valuable employees in such a situation when they get an opportunity to change jobs? Right again: They go away, don't they?

Now take this out of the context of an employer-employee relationship. What if the pusher is a husband whose wife is a sensitive? How many times can the pusher achieve personality comfort zone by going into emotion overdrive and dominating his wife—before she "goes away?" And spouses can "go away" in many ways other than divorce. In fact, they do so *more often* than divorce! That is the reason many, many marriages are sterile and unrewarding. All of us know it's possible to love someone without liking him or her very much...and that's tragic, isn't it?

Put a pusher on a fishing trip with three other men who are all potential friends, associates or customers. Now have it rain for the first two days of the three-day outing, and then make the first three bait shops they stop at "out of worms" when they get there.

Give this foursome a little hassle with the boat-rental people before they get on the water, and throw in a balky outboard motor just to add the final touch to the pusher's increasing discomfort.

He came there to fish. Two-thirds of his time has been wasted. The bait, the boat and the motor are all "bent nails" to him at this point. He goes into emotion over-ride; he is in critical personality discomfort.

The only way this person can return to personality comfort is to get about achieving his goal. To that end, he becomes bossy, dictatorial, curt. He will criticize anything and anybody who "wastes time" at this point. "C'mon, c'mon, Harry: Put that damn chart down and get this boat *moving,* willya?!"

Picture him in the bow of the boat, facing out toward the middle of the lake, his body-english actually trying to move the boat. Let's go, let's go!

How do the other three enjoy such a trip? When will they go with this person on another? What will they decide about becoming close friends or associates of this individual?

There is a tertiary stage of personality/reaction. The person goes into over-ride stage three when he's driven out of zone one (comfort) into zone two (reaction), and his automatic defenses don't work. He goes into stage or zone three: over-reaction. As we've seen, the pusher's hallmark in stage two is to become pushy, demanding, dictatorial. When this forces others to accede to him or her, the situation becomes personally comfortable to the pusher and he returns to stage one: his or her "normal" personality.

When the stage two reaction *doesn't* work, the mounting discomfort drives the pusher into stage three. This same principle applies to all four types; only the *reaction* is different. For the pusher, stage three over-reaction is identified by his sudden, and often sullen, "I quit."

How many times have you watched someone barking orders, demanding progress, becoming more and more argumentive and heated, and then suddenly:

"Oh, I don't care how you do it. I don't even care *if* you do it! I've had enough..."

The pusher stalks off, smoke rolling out of his ears, his jaw clamped shut. He's *mad*—and he has only one method left of trying to get back out of emotional discomfort: He *avoids* any further involvement in whatever it was—or with whoever it was—that pushed him through stage two into stage three.

Who Is The Examiner?

For openers, he's the fellow that frequently drives the pusher into stage two. The pusher likes short, concise statements of fact and he doesn't want to spend a lot of time. The examiner likes to "circle the wagon" before he lets go with an arrow. To him, the time spent discussing a project before it's begun is *important.*

The pusher's first question is "What are we going to do?"

The examiner's first question is "How we gonna do it?"

In fact, a first-class examiner would be concerned about *why* we're going to do something even before he gets to the part about *how* we're going to do it.

"We have to go over to the warehouse and move those widgets from aisle B to aisle C," the pusher says.

"How come?" the examiner asks.

"Because I said so," the pusher replies, already enroute to the warehouse; leaving the examiner standing there making a quick decision whether to (a) follow ther pusher, (b) tell him to kiss off, or (c) figure out why the widgets probably need to be moved.

If he's an employee, he'll probably follow the pusher, his mind going ninety miles a minute: By the time he gets to the warehouse he'll have a pretty good idea why the widgets need to be moved. When he finds out, later, that he was right, he will feel extremely pleased.

To anyone not an examiner, that probably sounds stupid: Why on earth did it *matter* whether he knew why? Did it have any bearing on moving the widgets? No; but to an examiner, it would have been important. Taking the time to explain why they had to be moved; and then how they were going to move them, would have made the examiner very comfortable. To the pusher it would have been time absolutely wasted.

While the pusher is *goal oriented*, the examiner is *procedure* oriented. The pusher wants (needs) to get the work done; the examiner wants (needs) to plan the work, then do it.

The examiner, critical of another person, would probably think something like this: "He could get a lot more work done if he did more pre-planning." It would surprise him and make him decidedly uncomfortable if he discovered that the other guy was probably thinking, about the examiner, "He could get more work done if he did less pre-planning and got on with it."

The examiner is the fellow who, when he was driving a nail into that one-inch, steel-backed board, would stop the work *right now* when the nail bent. "Huh! I wonder *why* that happened?" He might try one more and, when he got the same result, he would *immediately* begin trying to figure out what was wrong. He would not lift the hammer again until he had the answer!

Now we'd have this conversation between a pusher and an examiner:

"What's the matter? How come you're not driving nails?"

"It won't go in more than an inch," the examiner would say, "I'm trying to figure out what's wrong."

"Baloney!" The pusher would respond. "Gimmee that hammer!"

The examiner would stand by, quietly, and watch the pusher mangle several nails. When the pusher went through stage two into stage three and threw down the hammer (I quit!), the examiner would pick the hammer up and go back to trying to "figure out" what was wrong. By now, he'd have realized that the nail was going in one inch, the thickness of the board; and that there was something impervious behind it. He'd be well on his way toward deciding to get a drill or take some other approach.

If he was left alone long enough, he'd get the job done. Unfortunately, the examiner sometimes keeps worrying at the why and how of a job long after the job is no longer necessary. When time is of absolute importance to the value of a job, the examiner may lose much precious time planning...to a fault.

You can put an examiner into stage two by not giving him details and reasons for things, and then forcing him to act. He needs to plan, to be comfortable with the procedure. He's an A to B to C sort of person, and he doesn't work well—he's personality-stage-two —when he's forced out of his comfortable procedural methods.

How do you know when an examiner is in stage two? That's not always easy to spot with this person, because he or she is not given to expression, any more than is the pusher. With the pusher you can spot stage two fairly easily, because he or she becomes "pushy," authoritarian, demanding. The examiner's stage-two defense is to *avoid.* In a sense, this is very much a first cousin to the pusher's stage-three defense, the "I quit" syndrome. It's harder to spot it in an examiner, because he won't tell you through words or actions when he goes into "avoid mode." He'll just clam up.

The examiner withdraws his services simply by not doing any more thinking. That's right: His *principal* ability, and one he is very good at, is thinking things through. Give him scope and time, and he'll come up with some accurate and sensible ideas.

Put him into stage two by pushing him on a project or in a relationship, before he's ready, and he will mentally abandon the project or relationship. You may never see it happen, but you lost him or her right then—at least, as far as that particular episode is concerned. Do this to an examiner too often, and you've lost him or per...period.

Our language has an expression: "That person makes me do a slow boil..." —This expression is more properly labeled "property of the world's examiners," because that's what they do in "avoid mode," the stage two of personality discomfort. An examiner can get so angry in this stage that he or she is ready to boil over—and others around them would never see it.

Frequently, the first evidence you'll get that an examiner is in personality discomfort is when he or she goes into stage three. *Then* you'll know "something's up," for sure. In stage three the examiner becomes definitely autocratic, dominant almost to the point of brutality. He or she is, by nature, an excellent logistician; ordinarily articulate and capable of presenting a series of sword-swath denouncements that will "curl your hair."

You've heard the saying, "Boy, did he ever cut that guy down!" "Cutting somebody down to size" is a specialty of an angry examiner. He or she will use words and logic that will slash the opposition to ribbons. When an examiner is in stage three, you'll know it: He or she will be more like a pusher-type than the pushers will ever learn how to be.

If you're an examiner type, you'll remember those times when you said, "Okay, dammit! —*N*ow I'm mad!" Think about it for a moment: Weren't you really 'mad' before you got to that point? Why didn't you say so? —You didn't say so because you were in stage two when you started your slow boil: You were avoiding the contest, but not liking it. Whoever or whatever put you into stage two didn't leave you alone, however; the avoidance didn't work. So you went into stage three and "now" you're mad, and you act like it. Now the others will know, because you begin acting like a pusher.

Even if you "win" by changing the situation so that you can return to comfort zone one, you have probably really lost in the long run.

The examiner, driven to stage three, often overreacts so strongly that he or she destroys the personal relationships with those involved. Examiners in stage three are almost completely blind to the effects of what they may say or do. At that point, all they are trying to do is modify a *situation* by taking absolute control of it; in order to get things back to an environment comfortable for examiners.

Where the pusher is usually prone to conduct himself in a way in which the situation is more important than the people involved, he has at least *some* awareness of what he's doing to those people. When the examiner hits stage three, he loses virtually *all* awareness of what he's doing to those around him: He becomes totally goal-oriented. Get in his or her way at your emotional peril, when this happens.

This is the person who is eminently capable of analyzing all of the data available and then making a cold-blooded decision that the end justifies the means. "The means" are his or her primary involvement: Process and procedures are keys; once they've been analyzed the examiner makes his or her decisions about the goal. If an examiner is convinced that the "why" and the "how" can and should get the job done...it's all over. That job *will* get done.

Who Is The Sensitive?

You'll recall that the twin hallmarks of the sensitive are expressiveness and lack of assertiveness. This is the person we often think of as "mellow." The sensitive is usually well-liked, although pushers and outspokens will from time to time comment that the sensitive is "wishy-washy."

While the pusher is goal-oriented and the examiner is procedure-oriented, the sensitive is the first type we will look at who is *people*-oriented: To the sensitive, the human inter-relationships are more important than objects or circumstances.

Often the sensitive is considered a peace-maker; this is the person who goes about trying to patch up disputes between others (usually between pusher/examiner or pusher/ outspokens).

"Well, now—if you don't mind my comment, Charlie: Let's take a closer look at what John is saying, here. You two guys have been friends too long to be feeling upset about this..."

In a classic example, the sensitive couldn't care less about whether a job gets done, or how it gets done, so long as the people involved are in harmony and accord. There's little doubt the reason this person is sometimes thought of as wishy-washy is because he or she will vacillate about a decision until the interpersonal relationships are in order.

While others are demanding an answer on a course of conduct based on the situation's outline the sensitive will be trying to fit all the human relationships into the equation so that "nobody gets hurt"—only then is a sensitive comfortable with a decision.

While the examiner is often concerned with what others think of him or her, the sensitive is *usually* concerned with this. Often considered a dreamer, a follower, un-dynamic, nonproductive, still the sensitive is forgiven all of these "unfavorable" attributes because he or she is fun to be with, effervescent, and he or she "really cares" about people.

With someone this comforting, it's probably impossible to put them into stage two or three, right? —Wrong. *All* human beings go into personality override when they are forced out of their comfort zones. The sensitive is no exception to the rule: When the thinker can't operate comfortably, the emotion-factory kicks in, automatically, to try to adjust the situation back to stage one.

The sensitive's stage two is reasonably predictable, knowing what we know about his or her basic personality. Since it is interpersonal dynamics that force people into stage two, and since human relationships are the most important thing to this person, stage two would be the fastest possible route back to personal comfort: Everybody is happy again.

To achieve this, the sensitive gives in. Here again, we see the basis for the totally unfair criticism, "wishy-washy." The sensitive didn't give in because of defeat: He or she gave in because of the *other person's feelings*. The objective was not as important as the relationship, so the sensitive in stage two bartered his or her opinion or desire in exchange for the *other person's* emotional well-being. In this way, the sensitive achieves personality comfort zone one again: Everybody's happy.

The pusher, the examiner and the outspoken all would agree that the sensitive is "wrong" in his or her inordinate attention to human relationships. The others would all agree that sometimes you have to *do something* in spite of how other people feel about it.

Well, thank The Force for the sensitives among us: It would be a cold, dark world without these articulate, warm peacemakers. More than that: Can you think of a basic personality more appropriate for a loving spouse or parent; a loyal friend or employee—or boss?

What does the sensitive do if we push him or her through stage two into stage three? Well—first of all, how could we manage to do that? The sensitive, in stage two, gave in. Now how can we make him or her so uncomfortable that stage three sets in?

Consider a situation in which two people are arguing over the conduct of a job. The pusher wants to just get on with it—dammit!—because we're wasting time. The examiner is getting more and more uncomfortable because there hasn't been enough groundwork, enough planning. We don't have all the answers, yet. In this situation, the *sensitive* is the one who has to make the decision whether to press on or plan.

We put the sensitive into stage two when the others began to show hostility. At that point, our sensitive began to *try* to give in...but to which one? Of course, he or she had to somehow accede to both of the others; and this just wasn't possible. At first, the sensitive would try to make some face-saving, emotion-healing "deals:"

"Hey, John...Harry...look; can't we figure out how to maybe keep moving with some parts of this job while Harry checks on those areas that concern him? I mean, there must be something..."

"No way!" the pusher butts in. "We either get on with it or scrap it. We haven't got *time* to mess with Harry's nit-picking."

"Is that so?" Harry responds. "Look, if that's the

way you wanna run this outfit, that's fine with me. Just don't come to me later and cry about how this job came out..." (Notice that Harry is going into stage two, now: He's begun to avoid the situation; he's already mentally backing away from it.)

There's no way the sensitive can win in this mess: No matter what he or she does, the interpersonal relationships between John and Harry are going to deteriorate. So the sensitive is driven into stage three. What happens?

Right: In stage three, the sensitive is a wildcat. We've seen that the purpose of stage two and stage three is for the person to —somehow — regain situational control so he or she can return to operating in personality comfort. There's not much hope for gaining control in any situation if your first line of defense is to give in, when there are more than one or two others involved in a dispute. You can "control" a dispute if you are a party to it and there's only one other. You can hardly "control" a three or four-way argument by giving in.

So, in stage three, the sensitive takes control in an often-startling, abrupt personality shift. This, more than any other among us, is the Jekyll-Hyde personality; when the sensitive hits stage three it shocks those around him or her.

Ordinarily, the sensitive is kind and peaceful. In stage two he or she becomes even more tractable, usually while those around are becoming more hostile and combative. The others will begin more or less ignoring the sensitive as the dispute heats up. Suddenly, pow! The sensitive hits stage three:

"Okay, John and Harry: Both of you guys just shut up and sit down. I mean it! I don't have to sit here and listen to this, and I'm not going to. If you don't stop acting like two little kids, I'll take you both off this project—and that's a promise. Now, dammit! *You* listen to *me*..."

In this stage the sensitive will be projecting intense emotion. There will be no question in the minds of others that he or she is mad enough to spit nails and capable of doing exactly what is threatened. There is something almost instantly chastening to others involved when this happens. And that, of course, is the reason for the defense mechanism to operate precisely as it does: The situation is once again under control, the sensitive can go back to personality stage one, the comfort zone.

As soon as the others involved have been startled into paying attention, the sensitive reverts to stage one almost instantly:

"Look, I'm sorry I popped off at you guys. Doggone it, you're my two best salesmen. We need to work together on this project and I need both of you. Now, come on: Let's work it out..."

Who Is The Outspoken?

Here she comes, and people begin smiling in anticipation. She'll come through the restaurant like a small hurricane, slapping one person on the back; yelling "hi" to someone toward the rear of the room. "How's your old lady, Sam?" she'll ask one person as she breezes past, and before Sam can answer, the out-outspoken will inquire of the waitress, "Hey Louise —you gettin' any?"

When she gets to the table she'll drop into the chair (that someone else probably vacated for her) and immediately dominate the conversation. Would she ask the others what they had been talking about before she got there? —Are you kidding? What would *she* care? —Now that she's here, we'll talk about what *she* wants to...

The outspoken person is comfortable when he or she is at front stage center. This is true, to a certain extent, of the sensitive also; but with one major difference: The sensitive will give up being the center of attraction immediately when he or she senses that other people's feelings might be hurt. Not so the outspoken: This character seems to thrive on verbal contests. Give one of these folks an opportunity to "discuss" something, and they're off and running.

"That road out past the fairgrounds is sure nice since they blacktopped it," someone will say, and the outspoken pounces:

"Horse manure! They put more ripples in it than a damn washboard! Somebody ought to investigate that sweetheart of a paving deal—I'll bet there's some old payola in that setup. As a matter of fact..." (It's hard to write the probable end of this tirade, because the outspoken will continue at length—maybe changing the subject three times—before anyone else gets a word in.)

The outspoken is a natural interrupter, bouyantly and supremely happy that he or she has something to say—anywhere, on any subject—that the others ought to hear.

For the outspoken, personal comfort—stage one—is precisely that: Stage One. This person is goal-oriented as much as the pusher, and because he or she is so expressive, the outspoken runs a far higher risk of damaging interpersonal relationships for the sake of the job at hand.

These folks are the bane of the examiner's existence, because they are poles apart when it comes to planning and analyzing the situation. The outspoken is the person we all accuse of "going off half-cocked." This is true, because by nature, he or she is a doer; and a doer in extremes.

To put an outspoken into stage two is comparatively easy, and in stage two the outspoken person usually rapidly achieves personal control and quickly returns to stage one. This volatile individual is highly emotion-operated as a result of this volatility.

To him or her, time has equal importance as it has to a pusher...not your time, however: His or her time. The outspoken will happily sit and swap stories over coffee for a long time, paying no attention to the clock or to other's reasons for being there...until he or she decides it's time to "get on with it" (what?—anything at all: The outspoken is sometimes so goal-oriented he'll suddenly, compulsively, set out to "do something" even before he or she has a clear idea what that "something" is).

So: To drive this person into discomfort stage two; to evoke an emotional reaction, all we need to do is interfere with the outspoken's sense of time value, to get in the way when this person is "doing something," or deprive him or her of the center of attention for too long. Any or all of these will do the trick very nicely. And then what?

In stage two, the outspoken attacks. When he or she begins to lose the center, or the argument, you'll see this person begin to gesture even more hugely. The features become even more animated. The voice is raised and the choice of words becomes more pointed, more argumentive.

"No, no...wrong!...Sam, I'm *telling* you; now dammit, pay attention—there's only one way to handle this, and you're doing it wrong..."

Because this reaction—the attack—is usually quickly successful for the outspoken, he or she will go into and out of stage two rapidly. All that's needed for this person to operate in comfort stage one is that he or she be more or less in control of the situation and conversation. These folks don't necessarily have to be arguing to be comfortable: They can be in agreement; voluably, excitedly in agreement...and function just as well. The one thing they can't handle is to be either for or against, but made to be quiet and "out of it."

Suppose stage two doesn't work? Suppose the outspoken's "attack mode" doesn't get the job done? What happens when he or she goes into stage three?

Again, now that we know the purpose of both stage two and stage three is to (somehow) bring the situation back into the stage one comfort zone, we can almost predict how this person over-reacts to personality discomfort: By giving in. An outspoken in stage three is remarkably like a sensitive in stage two: He or she is apologetic, understanding and amiable.

The expressiveness is still there in stage three, although subdued; but the assertiveness is all gone, now. We now hear the outspoken "lose" an argument:

"Sure, sure, Mike...look, I'm sorry I got out of line. I didn't mean to make you mad or upset. Gee...I mean it, pal; come on, smile, willya?"

Almost childlike, the outspoken will resume his assertive, flambouyant mein almost instantly when the other person or people have "come around" to his peace-making overtures. He or she will be all sweetness and light in stage three, only to quickly go back to being aggressive as soon as it is possible to once again operate in comfort stage one.

Let's take one more look:

The pusher is assertive and unexpressive. He is goal oriented and has less concern for other people's feelings. When made uncomfortable, the pusher becomes dictatorial, authoritive. If that doesn't work, stage three defense is to avoid, to quit, to resign. (If I can't have my way, I won't play.)

The examiner is unexpressive and unassertive. This person is very analytical by nature; concerned with procedure and planning more than goals. More aware of other's feelings than the pusher, nevertheless the procedure and, ultimately, the goal are probably more important than individual feelings. Put the examiner in discomfort stage two and he or she will "avoid," usually in a way you won't immediately see: At first, the avoidance is internal, a "pulling away" from the situation. Driven to stage three, the examiner becomes assertive and dynamically authoritarian: He or she becomes a pusher with a vengeance. In this mode, the examiner is capable of doing lasting damage to personal relationships.

The sensitive is expressive and unassertive. This person is the peace-maker in the group. Always concerned with other people's feelings; the human aspect of any circumstance or relationship. Sometimes considered wishy-washy, unable to make up his or her mind. Not necessarily true: But the decision made will remain a secret while there's any chance of damaging a relationship by exposing the decision. You drive a sensitive out of comfort stage one into defense stage two by creating an interpersonal situation where there is animosity; where someone's feelings are jeopardized. In stage two the sensitive gives in, or tries to. If this doesn't work:

Stage three for the sensitive is to attack; often with breathtaking suddenness, and wholly out of character. The effect is startling and usually successful: The argument is ended because the lamb suddenly became a lion and scared the pants off everyone by roaring at them.

The outspoken is a joy to be with most of the time; a bit of a bore some of the time, but front-center-stage all of the time. Goal oriented, this person will take off to do a job before he or she clearly understands what the job consists of.

Dynamic, expressive and assertive, the outspoken entertains and produces restlessly, energetically. If you want a job done, give it to this person—especially if you're not sure what the job really is. He or she will begin whaling away at it, usually finding out halfway through where the problems are, if any.

He or she easily goes into stage two and just as easily recovers stage one because of it: Stage two for the outspoken is to attack, and ordinarily others involved will subside quickly, allowing the outspoken person to resume personality comfort. If, however, stage two is unsuccessful, these folks reverse the process of the sensitive: The lion becomes a lamb; the roaring ceases and the outspoken sues for peace.

These, then, are the four basic types of people in our world. Everyone will fit into one of these four categories. Sometimes the personality is less distinctly seen than with others: There are classic examples, and there are more subtle ones.

Earlier when we made a chart using one vertical and one horizontal "1 to 10" scales, we added lines so that each full quarter of the square was also broken into quarters. Remember the box? We made one big box with four parts, like this:

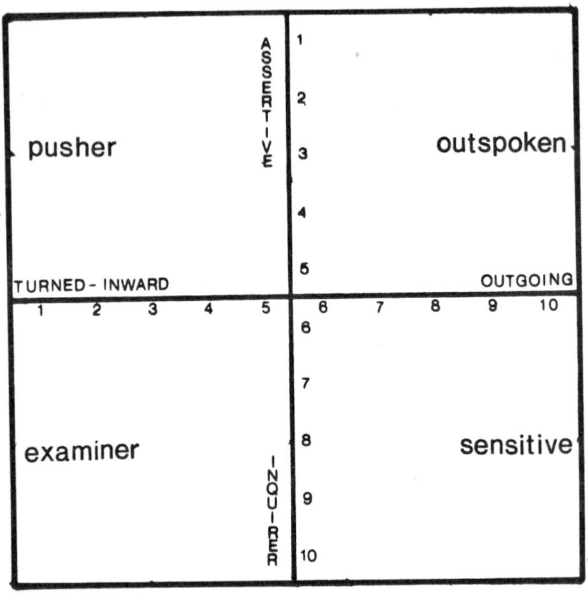

And then we split each of those quarters into four more quarters. Why'd we do that? —not everybody is a full-blown example of personality type. Some people will be predominately one type, with shadings of another thrown in. For our purposes, it's not really necessary to go into this in such depth that we could identify, for example, an "outspoken examiner" or an "outspoken pusher." (incidentally, those are the classifications of Steven Mariner and Dr. Bob Nara, in that order...)

We want you to be able to understand the four *basic* personalities and how they function emotionally. Everyone will fit one of these categories better than the other three, and that's his or her essential personality.

Which of the four is "better?" Definitely, absolutely and once-for-all: There is no such thing as a "better" way to be. Each type has advantages and disadvantages. Each of us has good points and bad points. It's not just wrong to think of one personal style as being superior to another; it is very likely damaging to make any attempt to change from one to another.

This, incidentally, is why so many "isms" making the rounds today are basically ineffective if not dangerous: Many of these so-called self help ideas want you to become something other than what you are. We are given a picture of a "perfect" personality, and then urged to emulate it. Well, if there was such a thing, it would be the best parts of all four types; doing away with the worst parts. It would call for someone who always functioned with cool reason and logic, who was never prey to his or her own emotion-factory...never went from comfort stage one into defense stage two or three.

There ain't no such animal; not on this side of an asylum fence, anyway. There may be people in various laughing academies, put away where they can't harm themselves or others, who are devoid of emotion—but they are not reading this book.

By now you've begun forming some conclusions as to which type you are; and probably you've thought about friends, spouse, co-workers. Do so! The more you think about this, the more you'll understand how it works...and the better you can learn to use the 180-Degree Theory to best advantage.

In no way did we help you learn about personality types so that we could help you change your own style. For openers, you probably can't do it; and for a conclusion: There's no reason to try; there's nothing wrong with the way you are. You may be a pusher, a sensitive, an examiner or an outspoken...and that's fine. What we *will* do, instead of trying to rebuild your basic self-structure, is help you become adept at living in it and using it to your fullest advantage.

Never again should you have to be victimized by some "system" that says you're a personality failure and then shows you how you can "become the life of the party." Nuts! If you were an outspoken to begin with, or perhaps a sensitive, you already *were* often the life of the party. If you're a pusher or an examiner, you weren't meant to be the life of the party. The fact that you have been once or twice, if you're a pusher or examiner, probably only proves the great personality-adjusting power of ethyl hydroxide—booze—right?

What these life-changing programs offer is much more than they really produce. You may change, a little bit for a little while, but it's neither a major or lasting change. When it fails to "measure up" to the promises made on the book cover, you add still another "failure" to your list and end up worse than before you began.

There are a few "isms" on the market which tell us it's all right to be what we are. Hooray for them! They couldn't be more to the point and the only fault with some of these approaches is that, once they've said it's okay to be you, they leave you no way to find out who you really are.

Well, you are a pusher, or an examiner, or a sensitive, or an outspoken. Whichever you are, good for you! Now, as you continue to learn about the 180-Degree Theory, hopefully much of your experience will begin to make a lot of sense to you. Many attitudes and numerous "quirks" in your personality will take on meaning. The bottom line is that we're going to help you go from an understanding of what you *are* to an ability to use your good points and dull the edge of your bad points.

It's as promised earlier: We have no intention of trying to make you over into something you *can't* be; we want you to be all you *can* be.

Chapter Four

"The Hidden Persuaders"

Earlier we more or less established that our thinking mind can be, and often is, heavily influenced by our non-thinking, emotional self. This of course is true of any personality type; it is partly the defensive reaction of the emotional subconscious that puts us out of our "comfort range" and into stages two and three—into reaction.

Also, we discussed how the cognitive (thinking) mind programs the subconscious, both for good and for bad; with the truth and with outright lies. We're going to go into this conscious programming technique in detail, later on; for now, we only need to remember that we do that to ourselves constantly, by accident: The 180-Degree Theory will help us to do it frequently *on purpose*.

What else programs the unconscious? We call these "the hidden persuaders" because they are just that: They are very persuasive, and we are almost never aware that we are being persuaded, programmed. We know what some of them are, don't we? —Society is one: The social structure we're born into, the surroundings which "feed back" to us constantly. What's another? —That's right: TV is a big influence; and that leads us into still another: Advertising.

High on the list of hidden persuaders would be our friends and associates. Of these, the closer the relationship, the more we are influenced by these others.

Some of the hidden persuaders go way, way back...into our developing years; even, according to many psychologists, to some beginnings of emotional reaction in the womb itself.

The effect of these influences is *conditioning.* We react to outside influence in either one of two ways: We *think* about what's happening; or we *feel* about it. When external influence comes against us suddenly, so that we notice it, the reaction is more likely to be cognitive. We are more likely to use our thinker when we are *aware* of a situation. When the external occurrence is more subtle, so that we aren't jarred into thinking, we are prone to react emotionally. *How* we will react depends upon two things, essentially:

1. What personality type we are, and
2. How we are subconsciously conditioned to handle this circumstance.

Want an example? Okay: Husband Joe comes home an hour and ten minutes later than he was expected. He, by the way, is a pusher. He comes through the door offering no excuse, no explanation. He is, or seems, "uptight" and a little bit angry.

Wife Eloise is a sensitive. She was concerned when Joe didn't come home. The later he became, the more she worried. Supper had been ready on time, was now getting cold, so Eloise did her best to keep the food fresh and warm at the same time...no mean trick, as many of us know. With time to think, she planned to ask him questions; to remind him that there are telephones...the whole nine yards.

As soon as Joe steps through the door, his face clouded, Eloise (a sensitive, remember) immediately forgets her questions and chiding. She's concerned about Joe's obviously upset feelings.

His greeting? "For the luvva Mike, Eloise—why isn't supper on the table?"

Her reaction? —confused guilt.

Eloise and Joe have had a relatively joyless marriage for several years. Both of them are vaguely aware that something is wrong, but they can't seem to articulate it, to discuss it. Eloise came from a family where the wife—her mother—was one of those efficient types who always had everything under control, the house immaculate and schedules run like a Swiss watch.

Her father was a quiet, thoughtful man. She never saw her parents argue—never. In her own marriage there are arguments, although not so frequently for the past few years, since she began giving in to avoid conflict. Joe dominates the marriage and has become subconsciously accustomed to always having his way.

If you add to the equation the programming of TV families and advertising, both of which tend to present an unrealistic "normal" household, you can see why Eloise never had a chance.

She's a sensitive, so she was concerned for Joe's feelings. She's programmed by her childhood to think of a wife and mother as "being on the ball." She's further programmed by voluntarily "losing" arguments until, subconsciously, she no longer has the capacity to truly defend, much less attack.

She was upset and tense, forced to operate out of her comfort zone. She was close to being in stage two before Joe even got home and when he did, his demeanor "tightened the screws" even further. His uncalled-for remark about the meal triggered her automatic, unconscious reaction. She went into full stage two which, for a sensitive, is to give in.

—Give in to what? The demand was there, but it was quite subtle, because it wasn't verbalized. In complaining about the supper, Joe was, in effect, telling Eloise she couldn't live up to her own ideals as a home-maker. The only way for her to give in, to that, was to agree subconsciously.

She was confused, because—somewhere, way in the back of her mind, her thinker was trying to tell her that she hadn't done anything wrong. And she was guilty, because she wasn't living up to the standards that had been impressed upon her subconscious mind as a child.

In this scenario, there are two highly-probably outcomes. Eloise will mollify Joe, serve the meal, and the tension will subside. It will leave a scar on Eloise; a little one, true, but the cumulative effect of these can be like slow poison.

The other likely outcome is that Joe will continue to pick at her, not giving her a chance to get out of stage two. The confusion and guilt will keep mounting along with the tension until—Whammo! Eloise, a sensitive, goes into stage three and attacks like a banshee. Now we have a fullblown knock down, drag out argument. Want to continue this scenario to its conclusion?

Okay: Joe is a pusher, right? He'll go into stage two when Eloise attacks and become autocratic, demanding, pushy. The contest will get louder and more painful. Eloise is in stage three and locked; no chance for her to get out of it with Joe piling on the pressure. Finally, Joe will join her in stage three, and he's only got one "out" when that happens: He quits, he avoids completely.

As we leave this tranquil domestic scene, Joe has just thrown his fork down on the plate and stomped out the door. Eloise is sitting at the table, head down, crying.

They were both the victim of *feelings*, not thinking.

The hidden persuaders in our lives add up to a personal filtering system, in which the truth (reality) is filtered through a set of values unique to each of us, and comes out colored and modified by those values. Any policeman will tell you that if there are five witnesses to a crime, there are likely to be five startlingly different descriptions of the suspect—and five completely different stories about what happened.

Reality, the unmodified facts and events (circumstances) of our lives, is the *only* input our cognitive mind can work with to come up with *realistic* decisions. The coloring of facts which we all do, all the time, comes from our set of conditioned values which are *subconscious*, they are *conative* (feelings), they operate *continuously*, and they are *almost always incorrect.*

This becomes easy to grasp, this predisposition to error, when we realize that the conative or subconscious mind has to "bend" reality until its shape coincides with our conditioned values. Sometimes this re-shaping is minor, because the facts are quite close to what we'd like them to be, subconsciously. In these cases, the error is small; probably not significant.

But what happens when the unconscious mind has to do *a bunch* of tailoring on reality in order for it to fit our unconscious value-set? In such cases as the latter, the modification of reality will be very significant, and any decisions we make about this particular set of "real" circumstances *will be as incorrect as the amount of subconscious tailoring.*

We've talked, earlier, about General Custer's decision to surround 6,000 Indians with 250 soldiers. History assures us that the general was told about "many Indians" gathered at Little Big Horn. He had the facts. He knew how to use them; or he wouldn't have been a general officer.

How could he have been so wrong? History gives us no clue, except for a tantalizing, little-known fact which took place just before this incident—we'll re-visit this episode again, in a later chapter, and unveil that fact.

One conclusion we could make was that somebody very badly advised the general: *Somebody* gave him some "bum dope." Who was that somebody?

We have every reason in this world to suspect that the "somebody" who screwed up the facts was none other than George Armstrong Custer; the last man we'd have expected to make such a screwball value judgment. And we have every reason in this world to suspect that where the warping of reality into desire took place was in the intermixing of cognition (reality) and conative process (subconscious desire/feelings) inside his mind.

In case the reader is wondering what an episode in 1876 has to do with us, more than 100 years later, let's focus on the issue: Whenever your own subconscious feelings can so interfere with your thinking that you're convinced you can beat odds of 24-to-one, *you need the 180-Degree Theory.*

Fact: There are "thousands" of Indians at Little Big Horn. They're hostiles, and they are ready to fight.

Fact: You have 250 officers and men under your command.

Conclusion?

Factual: 24-to-1 odds are not condusive to success. We'll wait until things are a bit more favorable; meanwhile the scouts can keep an eye on the Indians.

Emotional: 250 well-trained and well-armed men ought to be more than enough for a few thousand poorly-armed wild Indians...especially under *my* command...Now's my chance!

The hidden persuaders have been conditioning us since before birth and they'll be "at us" until we shuffle off. It simply isn't possible to shut out the pervasive, persuasive information which we're bombarded with constantly. We have only one chance, and that is to learn how to control our decision-making process so that we allow as little emotional error as possible.

How many women in this country today are prodded by vague feelings that their marriages are less than successful, when every scrap of real, factual information they have tells them they shouldn't be "feeling" slightly unhappy and restless? There could be many reasons for this—there are many reasons for this—but let's just look at one possible hidden persuader that could be responsible: TV advertising.

We won't compile a list; we'll just take one specific product and think about it: Furniture polish.

Now...what possible impact can furniture polish have on subconscious feelings about a marriage?

Think about the TV advertising for such products. Generally, they show a proud, contented woman bragging about how she gets a beatiful shine with no effort because she uses Brand A; or maybe the younger wife is having trouble with greasy dust on her furniture until the wise older woman turns her on to Brand B, after which bliss eternal reigns.

Will buying and owning a spray can of Brand A or Brand B (or both) relieve the tensions such hidden persuasion can create, repeated over and over again? Don't bet on it. Why?

The point we miss (because the Ad agencies want us to miss it) is that the furniture in the house, and the house itself, are all beautiful and expensive. Incidentally, that describes the women in the ads, too: Beautiful and expensive.

Whether you buy Brand A or B or a dozen different cans of wax and use them three times a day, you can't escape the persuasion of the stage setting in these TV ads. The persuasion to buy the wax is an open persuasion, and you can handle that easily with your cognitive mind: Do I want a can of that stuff, or don't I?

The persuasion of the stage setting is hidden, and it's potent. You can't handle it with your cognitive mind, because *it has nothing to do with the reality of your life.* But it *will* program and condition your subconscious. Many psychologists would agree that buying the product only intensifies the hidden and unfulfilled feelings generated by the house beautiful/life beautiful ad.

Your subconscious cannot perceive between reality and truth. It is an idiot; it believes anything it is told. TV viewing impacts, to a huge degree, *directly* on the subconscious: TV producers and ad agencies intentionally use programming which requires virtually no cognitive thinking on the part of the viewer; therefore they have a pipeline right to the center of the unconscious.

Your idiot subconscious serves up a "feeling" to your conscious mind that you should buy a can of Goop furniture polish *because it will make you feel like the lady in the ad.* When you *do* buy it you get an immediate "buzz" of good emotion; your feelings have been "stroked." Of course, that *reinforces* the conditioning; and when using the polish doesn't have the emotional effect your idiot subconscious wanted it to have, the craving for fulfillment becomes even stronger.

In this one, tightly-focused example, it's easy to come up with the solutions:

(a) Buy $10,000 worth of furniture; a $75,000 home to put it in, and a $1.98 can of Goop Furniture Polish to use on it. Then you'll "feel better."

(b) Look the TV right into its one glaring eye, during these commercials, and say to it: "Uh-uh, sweetie—I know what you're trying to do. Forget it!" (Incidentally, if you want the can of wax, go ahead—it'll probably do your furniture some good. It won't make it new and expensive, but it'll make what you have just that much better...)

One aspect of the scenario we just examined is worth taking a closer look: The reinforcement of "feelings" by acting upon them. We're going to devote more time to this in a later chapter, but while it's still fresh in your mind from the furniture polish caper, think about this, please.

Every time we do something without knowing clearly *why* we do it, we're operating to some degree under the direction of the subconscious mind. A classic illustration is rearranging the table service when we sit down in a restaurant. Nearly everybody does this, almost every time. Why? Do we say to our selves, "I'd like that ashtray nearer the center of the table; the salt and pepper shakers more to the right but closer to my side, and the napkin a bit more off to the left?"

Of course we don't "say that to ourselves" —Or do we? *Something* tells us to do it. What else but the unconscious mind, for motives only it can perceive? The point is that once we've done it, we *immediately feel better.* And, if you doubt that doing reinforces feeling, the next time you go into a restaurant, try *not* moving the table service...

Minor "quirks" like this aren't important. It will have virtually zero effect on your life if you do or do not move things around on the table. Such small habit patterns are so far buried in the subconscious mind as to be nearly on the same level as breathing and yawning. Let's not get caught up in trying to run the autonomous "plant maintenance" section; we're involved in the communications department, the information-handling components of our mind-computer.

In this area, where it has an impact on our lives, we need to be aware that performance of an act demanded by our feelings will automatically reinforce those feelings, even though our conscious mind is trying to warn us that the action is not in our best interests.

When the cognitive mind is clearly in charge and we fully understand the situation, we can often shout down our feelings and avoid an action we ought not perform. *Not* performing it *decreases* the feelings: We won't have nearly as tough a time making the decision the next time we're faced with it.

> Action reinforces feelings; inaction (other action) weakens feelings.

Where we often have trouble is on the occasion when our cognitive mind is not crystal clear on the circumstances. In these cases, we have a "still, small voice"' trying to tell us to take a 180-degree turn, to ignore our feelings. That small voice, of course, is *intuition.* Although it seems quite a bit like feeling or emotion, intuition is a bona-fide member of the cognitive family: It is *not* an idiot; it is knowledge arrived at without conscious thinking, but it is still *knowledge.*

Whenever intuition vies with emotion, *go with the intuition.* The most dangerous thing in these cases is to follow the mis-advice that, "if it feels good, do it;" because just as surely as you "do it," you'll reinforce emotional feelings and weaken intuition. If the same situation repeats often enough (and it doesn't take very many repititions), the intuition is silenced and feelings are fortified.

The outcome, in that set of conditions, is that you will always make your decision to do or not to do based on the desires of an idiot (your subconscious) instead of the knowledge of an intelligent person (yourself). And, every time you do the wrong thing because of this situation, you'll immediately *feel better* about it. You get an instant "rush" of well-being that builds up your feelings' ego dynamically.

In just about everyone's life, there is some area which is out of control because of this. We articulate it something like this: "I know I probably shouldn't do that, but I *just can't help myself!*"

Why would a young, attractive, intelligent woman allow herself to be picked up for a one-night-stand, again and again; hating herself for it the next day but virtually unable to put on the brakes...even though she's destroying her chances for happiness?

—Because she "just can't help herself," right?

Awareness of the hidden persuaders in our lives is power to help defeat the bad ones. We will seldom know we are being persuaded at the exact moment when it's happening. It is insidious, sneaky; it impacts on our subconscious and adds to the memory banks loaded with faulty information, ready to be served up to our conscious mind.

Since we can't usually prevent the acquisition of this faulty data, these hidden persuaders, our only line of defense is the continual realization that our subconscious *is being hoaxed* and that it is, therefore, unreliable as an adjunct to decision-making.

We do this defensive thinking whenever we're faced with conflicting "urge" as opposed to "reason." Our defense consists almost completely of understanding that we have been misguided in the past, are being misguided today, and will be tomorrow, in ways which we cannot control. This understanding helps us come up with the strength of will to ignore feelings and follow reason more often than not.

We learn more and more to think of the subconscious "feelings" as the immature tantrums of an idiot; one which is constantly teased and tempted by hidden persuasion.

A child watching TV can become persuaded he will "feel better" if he has a specific brand of sugar-coated yummies. To this end, he pesters you in the store; throwing a tantrum if necessary. So you buy the yummies; *immediately* the kid is happy (a rush). He probably doesn't eat the whole box: The "promise" was more than the reality, and he gets no *real* satisfaction from it. But the syndrome was reinforced, so when TV persuades the youngster that he'd be happy with a different color or shape of sugar-coated yummies, we go around again.

In that little story, the child is *your subconscious;* the tantrum in the store are *your feelings*, and the purchase of the valueless junk food against your better knowledge is *giving in to feelings.*

Unless you want to go through life giving good value for sugar-coated promises which cannot deliver satisfaction; with this losing proposition reinforced every time it happens, you need to defend against the hidden persuaders around you.

Let's modify today's "advice" so that it makes more sense, to help you remember that your feelings have been programmed without your permission:

"If it feels good, *watch out!*"

—And remember the 180-Degree Theory: If there's any doubt, turn about—and run like the dickens.

Chapter Five

"My Mother Made Me Do It"

Mothers of the world have been getting "bad press" for years because of a man named Sigmund Freud. Perhaps especially in the United States, where psychoanalysis has been one of the favored party pastimes for at least two generations, we tend to look for the psychological roots of our current troubles somewhere in our formative past.

Stuttering...? Bedwetting...? Fingernail chewing...? —Somewhere, sometime, while your psyche was young and tender, Mama did something to you (or withheld something from you); and that was the root-cause of the difficulty.

Do you often dream about Christmas trees? A Freudian psychologist/psychiatrist might ponder the symbolism: Trees are male phallic symbols; ornaments, vases and the like may well be vaginal symbols. Somewhere in your dream of Christmas trees lurks the murky sex/parents/id-ego center of your problems...if only we can make any sense of the symbolism.

If lay people at times furrow the brow in puzzlement at these far-out "explanations," they are increasingly in good company: Many counselors and researchers are beginning to question validity of this approach. It may be a form of heresy, but the question demands recognition: "What if the Christmas-tree dreamer just happens to like Christmas trees because they make him/her 'feel good?'"

One of the things that takes place during a long-term analysis where such things as balls and vases are discussed is a long-term *conversation* between counselor and counselee. They talk. The counselor (if he's any good) listens; and the kind of listening he/she does is the kind that inspires trust and evokes confidences.

It may be that a truly competent doctor can piece the Freudian puzzle together, given long enough, and come up with the answers for a patient. It may also be that, given the same amount of time, the patient/doctor relationship provides a vehicle in which the *patient* comes up with the answers simply by having a sympathetic audience which helps him/her draw the answers out of hiding from the unconscious.

Are we saying, then, that the entire school of Freud-based psychoanalysis is worthless? No, we're not: The contributions made by Freud and later researchers/practitioners following his lead are invaluable. We are bucking against only one theme that has its roots in Freudian theory: That "what we are" is set in concrete early in life, and that *we cannot change, without unlocking the secrets of the past.*

What we can't change is our basic self-structure; our personality type. Sometime early in each life we begin to coalesce into the individual we will be for the balance of our lives; whether 'pusher,' 'examiner,' 'sensitive' or 'outspoken.' These personality traits are extremely visible, for example, on a grade-school playground.

Mr. Freud *et al* are probably very close to the truth in their understanding that such personality styles are created, virtually irrevocably, very early in life. Your mother, in other words, made you what you are—together with your father, brothers and sisters, aunts and uncles, schoolteachers, genes, environment, society, and the TeeVee.

What this theory missed, apparently, was that we *can* change the way we behave...or, to put that differently, we can modify the way we react to things around us. The "old guard" in psychology said that the only way we could change our behavior was to understand what caused our present behaviour—to go back to our formative years and unlock the keyways of the mind; to learn *precisely why* we react the way we do.

The "next guard" (behoviorists) said Freud was bonkers. "Nuts," they said, "We can do with people what we do with rats in the laboratory: We can *make* them change their behavior."

How did they do this?—The same way they did it with those rats, by repetitive conditioning. For example, there's a reasonable assumption that you could cure thumb-sucking by rigging up a battery-operated device that gave the thumb-sucker a shock every time he touched his thumb to his lips. Whether he'd then turn to wetting the bed is a question for Dr. Freud, who unfortunately is no longer with us.

Freudian theory would cure the thumbsucker by digging into his deep past and deep sexual drives to find out *why* he sucked his thumb.

Behaviorists would figure out some way to condition him so that he *had to* stop sucking his thumb.

The 180-Degree Theory would achieve its purpose by helping him *want* to stop sucking his thumb.

Freudian analysis often works, but it's the "long way home," and anyone who truly needs long-range psychiatric care isn't going to get relief from this or any other self-help book. If a person is sick enough to need a physician, he or she isn't going to recover with a paperback copy of the "Home Medical Advisor." And if a person is mentally sick enough to need a doctor, he or she ought to make an appointment today.

Behaviorism also works, but there is something obscene about the concept, which goes by another name: Mind Control. There is reason to wonder if external conditioning on the scale of behaviorism won't eventually lead to mental complications more severe than the "behavior" the conditioning alters. Behaviorists can take an *examiner* and turn him/her into an apparent *outspoken*. Viola! —A different person emerges!...What happens to the "old" person? Where does he/she go? —Isn't it possible, even likely, that the "old person" is still prowling in the hallways of he subconscious, plotting and scheming ways to stage a comeback?

None of us needs a split personality. We all have enough to cope with, simply keeping our natural personality on the right course...which is usually 180 degrees from what we "feel" the right course to be. Nobody needs the added complication of sorting out two different sets of compass headings coming up from the subconscious.

A major point: Personality type has no bearing on the cause or cure for self-image problems; or on the way we're touched by life around us. The only difference personality type makes is *how* the problems affect us; and *how* we perceive the reality of life. There is not a shred of reason to wish your basic self-structure, your personality, were something different than it is. And that's a good thing; because there's no way short of mind-blowing trauma, insanity, or laboratory-rat conditioning, that you can change what you *are*. You *can* change—within reason—what you *do* with what you are.

Doubletalk? —Not at all: You can completely remodel a building without changing the walls or foundation, can't you?

The 180-Degree Theory is a variant of behavior-modification, with one vital and all-important difference: The full-fledged behaviorists re-program part of the autonomous "computer" —the subconscious —to achieve the desired habit shift. This does nothing about the *system*. It's the same "tape deck," playing back a different tape.

The 180-Degree Theory provides the means for altering the system, so that the subconscious is continually programmed and re-programmed by the conscious mind.

Behaviorism changes parts of your subconscious, but still leaves it far too much in control: You are still operated by your feelings, albeit now in a different direction than before. The 180-Degree Theory puts the *conscious* in control, allowing for a constantly-monitored program that changes former direction as often as necessary to realize the desired results.

The "trick"' we are going to steal from the behaviorists is *intentional habit shifting.* Since habit is nothing more than an automatic or semi-automatic response of the subconscious to stimulus from outside, it stands to reason that the boss computer, the conscious, can over-ride these responses. There's no doubt, anymore, that this repetitive over-ride *will* change habit patterns.

We're going to stop emphasizing "why" we mis-cope with certain life situations. We can safely assume that Freud was at least partly right, that experiences earlier in life set the stage for the way we react. So what? Even if you went through extensive, expensive therapy and ultimately discovered exactly what traumatic experience(s) in childhoold cause you to react erroneously, what would you gain?

—You'd gain encouragement, initiative and will to change your reaction program. Knowing "why" helps you believe you can overcome the situation. It's also likely at least in some cases that re-living the traumatic experience as an adult will burn out the old subconscious programs (which are a child's) and replace them with a new program—one that more closely matches the reality of today.

Burning out the old programs —cauterizing them with the searing pain of trauma—really works. Here again, it works for *one specific program* and does nothing to amend the incongruity of being governed by the subconscious...a child, an idiot.

We are going to begin emphasizing "what" we do wrong, not why we do it. Understanding our errors in coping with life is something the conscious mind can handle very easily. We are *usually aware* when we've mis-coped...screwed up...blown it. We say to ourselves, "Boy, did I ever mess that up. I *always* seem to react like that in that situation! I wonder *why* I do that...?"

Do you see the progression? The conscious mind reacted to a reality it perceived: We just blew it. So far, so good...and then, we make the first mistake:

"I *always* seem to react like that..." Brother, that's just like patting your idiot subconscious on the head and telling it, "You done good, kid!" The *feelings* that lead to the reactive error have been forcefully energized. If you told a computer to "always do this," you may rest assured that it will always do precisely what you told it to.

Then we go off on a wild-goose-chase, trying to establish in our conscious mind the reason *why* our subconscious mind is feeding us course-of-conduct error. *Who cares why?* However, in becoming involved in this psychological fishing trip, we effectively remove our conscious mind from the task it ought to be performing: Identifying precisely *what* we did wrong and then re-programming the subconscious so that the same mistakes aren't repeated.

There is only one overall reason for reacting to given conditions in a pre-programmed manner: Our "feelings" (emotions) modify the reality of the situation so as to fit the subconscious mind-set, the preconceived, stored information about these or similar conditions.

The emotions mix with the cognitive thought on the matter and the resulting mixture is something like reality; it is now our perceived reality. We act upon this personalized view of reality; often to our detriment.

Here's the way we *should* have handled recognition of a mistake:

"Boy, did I ever mess that up! Come to think of it, I've generally reacted just about like that in that situation. Well, that's enough of that! I could care less *why* I seem to handle this situation in this manner: The only thing I'm genuinely interested in is that I don't do it like that again."

Now, this won't change your programming overnight. In fact, the next time you encounter similar conditions, your subconscious will probably serve up the same mixture of emotional mish-mash it "always has." The difference, of course, is that your *conscious* mind has ordered the system to put a red flag on this set of circumstances; one that says, "To be handled only by the Boss."

It will probably present itself as "intuition" when it surfaces. You'll "feel" two things: The emotional tug of your subconscious programming, and the quasi-emotional "still, small voice" of intuition.

"Go this way!" Your subconscious will cry out.

"Be careful!" Your intuition will admonish.

The signal from your intuition is enough to make you pause, to reflect, to remember, and to *think.* Once you begin using your conscious mind to analyze the data, minimizing the emotional input from your subconscious, you are usually able to make the best choice of action, the best decision.

Making a decision, by the way, is the function of the conscious mind *only*. The subconscious is incapable of making a decision; all it knows how to do is repeat a set of directions it learned earlier—sometimes many, many years earlier. The choices; the alternatives, are solely the property of the conscious mind.

There's an important thought here, one we should all try to remember all the time: Decisions are the final mental act prior to physical action. *Nothing* happens until we make a decision, aside from allowing our idiot subconscious take control and put us on fully-automatic response. There is one decision none of us make often enough: We can decide *not to decide anything*—until we've given it more thought.

Life hands us circumstances every day in which we are *apparently* required to make a decision. As soon as this happens, we begin to react to the external pressure. We *feel* that we have to do something, the sooner the better. Our idiot subconscious begins to throw several tantrums simultaneously: "Do this! No, do that! No, wait a minute...do this, instead!"

The external events are awaiting our action. Our

subconscious is screaming at us to do something. The only thing we *may* have going for us at this point is our friend intuition, who is muttering, "Man, I don't *want* to do anything just yet!"

Remember that there is one activity that is the final mental checkpoint preceding physical action: A decision has to be made by the conscious mind. We would all be far better off in life if we made one decision more often:

"Full hold! *No* action until I get more data, and *that's an order!*"

The ability to do this is the reason the 180-Degree Theory works; and we are going to continue learning how to take command of our mental destiny as the book unfolds.

There are two things we should examine in this chapter, because they are counter to the goal of learning to decide with our conscious mind.

One of these culprits is called "compulsion," the other is autonomous reaction.

Compulsion and autonomous reaction are similar in that neither of them has much to do with the conscious, rational mind. They're also similar in that they are "out of control," which is to say that the conscious mind probably can't prevent a course of action dictated by either compulsion or autonomous reaction.

Examples of the latter are breathing, heartbeat, digestion, etc. These are all neuro-physical programs that are designed to operate whether we "will" them to or not. We can control some neuro-physical functions, within tolerable limits: By an act of will, we can decide not to urinate—no matter how much we "have to go"—until the neuro-physical computers are forced to over-ride our willpower. One milliliter more than absolute capacity and—it's all over, no matter where we are or how much we'd really rather not "do that."

Some physical erectile tissues can abruptly mutiny against our conscious will, also. When this happens, our society's polite fiction that men have no external reproductive organs, or that women's breasts are melon or egg-shaped without any protrusions, is abruptly shattered—much to our dismay and embarrassment.

Generally, neuro-physical, autonomous reactions (or actions) are for our physical benefit. We'd be dead without them. There are cases in which the autonomous system causes problems, however: Nervous tics are an example, as is stuttering, uncontrollable sneezing or hiccups. A more devastating example is trigeminal neuralgia, the malady known as tic doloreaux, one of the most painful nervous disorders known to humanity (and apparently only to humanity, incidentally).

For our purposes: If your own autonomous system is functioning well enough to keep you alive, relatively comfortable and usually free of embarrassment, there's nothing you can or should do to change it.

If there is a problem with your autonomous system, it is more likely than not something you'll need trained, competent assistance to overcome. However: Sometimes automatic physical "difficulties" are evidence of psychological problems not severe enough to be considered disorders calling for professional help.

What has happened in the past is that people following the 180-Degree Theory (although they may not have called it that) have so improved their ability to cope with reality; have so increased their own self-esteem, that the neuro-physical "quirk" associated with that particular ego-problem just "went away."

—Are you disgusted with yourself because you knaw at your lip...or do you gnaw at your lip because you're disgusted with yourself? Either way: Learn not to be disgusted with yourself. Maybe you won't immediately stop eating at your lip, but you'll sure feel a lot better about it, won't you?

The other out-of-control system is compulsion. As a generality, there won't be much you can do about compulsion without help. Compulsion is, if not insanity, certainly a form of un-sanity. People who gamble, who are incapable of resisting gambling even though they are "tearing themselves up" with remorse and guilt, are compulsives. Alcoholics are compulsives.

Commonly accepted language for this condition is that the person can't help him/herself. As with many common beliefs, this is near the mark: The individual probably cannot overcome the compulsion without help; therefore can't "help himself." Help ranges all the way from being institutionalized to simply having someone listen sympathetically.

A classic illustration is Alcoholics Anonymous, the layman's organization devised some thirty years ago to help cope with compulsive alcoholism. In all of the years since its inception, nothing has come along more successful than A.A. Many A.A. theories and catch-phrases are applicable to other kinds of compulsion. One such A.A. saying sums up, beautifully, the principle that you cannot control a compulsion with the conscious mind, by an act of will:

"Alcoholism," they'd tell you, "is a disease. If you think alcoholics are simply weak-willed, try will-power on diabetes...or diarrhea!"

Again, as with autonomous systems, compulsions are the stuff from which psychologists' incomes derive. There is little in the 180-Degree Theory that will directly operate against an out-and-out compulsion. Most victims of this disorder, sooner or later, will have to face up to the fact that they aren't going to make it on their own.

Equally true, however, is the fact that the underlying cause of compulsions can sometimes be corrected *without ever knowing what the causes were* (Sorry about that, Dr. Freud). As with nervous tics and lip-chewing, thumb-sucking and other neuro-physical difficulties, compulsions can and often do simply evaporate when the individual begins to learn how to cope with life better; thereby gaining self-approval.

One cold November morning some thirty years ago a young man (12 or 13) was helping his father cut a length of wellpipe with a hacksaw. Bill's job was to hold the pipe so it didn't bind on the saw, while his powerful farmer father plunged the sawblade into the steel.

The third of fourth time the pipe slipped in Bill's hands his exasperated and temperamental father screamed at him, "You aren't worth the f--- it took to get you!"

Now in his 40's, Bill is a successful hospital administrator—too successful. In fact, he probably won't live to see his 50th birthday. He attacks his job like he attacked high school and college: He has a compulsive need to be not just "good," but good enough to prove to his father that he is and was "worth the f---" which conceived him.

If Bill went for help...if he recognized that he had a problem to begin with...there's a chance that an analyst might be able to take him back to that farmyard on that cold November day and let him see, as an adult, what happened to him as a child. In that viewpoint, he would be able to understand that he had achieved more than enough—he cold learn to relax.

Incidentally, Bill is the co-author's cousin and Steve Mariner was there, that November morning. It really happened; as did Bill's subsequent career in administration. Bill was and is brilliant, and he did come relatively close to killing himself with driving, compulsive ambition.

However, it's doubtful that he consciously remembers that childhood incident. He never sought psychiatric help; never even admitted to himself that he "had a problem." Instead, he was working one day (at the hospital, fortunately) when he suffered a major heart attack.

An adult trauma shoved the childhood trauma completely out of the picture: With his training and experience, Bill knew exactly what would happen to him if he didn't change his pace. His "thinker" took over from his subconscious. His feelings of having to do more, more, more were over-ridden by his knowledge that if he did, it would kill him.

Bill never heard of the 180-Degree Theory. In a way, that's too bad...because practicing it saved his life, his marriage and his career.

The 180-Degree Theory can't "cure" compulsive or autonomous behavior. If we made that claim, any reasoning person would stop reading right here and now—and should. If your *immediate goal* is to cure a compulsion, see a "shrink." And if you want to "cure" automatic reflex, see a Yoga Master.

You'll have to make the decision...remembering that the word "decision" *requires* that you *think* your way through, not simply rely on your emotional response. If you have a problem serious enough to be classed as a disorder, you might want to seek help. It's not a bad idea in any case.

Perhaps your compulsion(s) are borderline; you aren't as out-of-control as, for example, an alcoholic or a compulsive gambler. You may want to continue developing your knowledge and practice of the 180-Degree Theory, applying this technique to overcoming your individual compulsive-type behavior. If so, an observation is in order:

Compulsive and/or automatic behavior frequently —usually—stems from hidden anxiety. While they have the same source, the words anxious and anxiety have subtly different, and important, meanings. Anxiousness is something we all experience at times, and usually we realize, at the time, that we *are* anxious. Anxiety is more insidious. It seems to be anxiousness repressed or unfulfilled, shoved into the subconscious and not specifically thought about or identified. As a point of interest, the word-source for anxiety is the Latin word for "choked" —repressed.

Anxiety, in the subconscious, is like an infected scab on the skin. It won't heal by itself; if anything, it will get worse. This builds pressure on the psyche: Whenever any parts of our physical or neurological systems are out of order, *some* reaction will set in. So long as the subconscious "feels something wrong" it will try to compensate. The form often taken, in this compensation, is a compulsion or an automatic habit such as lip-gnawing.

Seldom is there any rational connection between the source of anxiety and the method by which we compensate. For reasons known only to itself, the subconscious selects a course of action to "blow off steam" and relieve the anxiety.

If, through an act of intelligent reasoning, we identify irrational, compulsive-type behavior; and through an act of rational will and implementation of the 180-Degree Theory, we manage to do away with the compulsion...

...won't the subconscious simply select another method of blowing off steam?

That's quite likely; it's also possible that the next way the subconscious selected would be closer to the real source of anxiety. In any event, if the individual *could* overcome such behavior without assistance, the anxiety source may not be either deeply ingrained, or severe enough to warrant professional help.

In such a condition, the pressure would simply begin to build up again when the behavior "relief valve" was tied down. That may be a "guts ball" way of looking for another leak in the pressure-system, but it would probably work. There's always the consideration that the anxiety itself would diminsh as self-image and coping ability improved.

After you've finished this book; after you're convinced that you understand and can apply the 180-Degree Theory, you will have taken a rather thorough personal inventory.

Based upon that inventory, you'll decide whether you "have a problem" requiring assistance...or whether you can work it out yourself, with the help of a good listener.

Incidentally, finding a good listener isn't easy. If you are fortunate enough to have a listener among your associates, by all means use him or her. If not; if you can't find a good listener, you can always rent one.

They're called counselors. A good one is worth every dime he or she is paid. If you know anyone who is a professional counselor, ask him or her how many times a new client begins the initial contact by saying something like, "If I don't talk to *somebody*, I'll go nuts..."

People don't mean that, of course: They could "talk to" anybody—spouse, co-worker, bartender, hairdresser—you name it. What they mean, of course, is:

"If I don't talk to *somebody who will listen*, I'll go nuts."

In a later chapter, we'll discuss listening. It's something that almost nobody does well but, surprisingly enough, it's something that almost anyone can learn to do very well, indeed.

Behavior of any sort aside from significant compulsion or autonomous reaction will yield to the conscious mind. Even borderline compulsions and habits can be brought under control by an "act of mind."

The key principle of this chapter, then, is that we need to discover *what* we are doing wrong—not *why* we're doing it. The identification of our personal "goofs" is something we can handle consciously, with our cognitive powers. We can weigh factual evidence, examine actual conditions and circumstances, and draw reasonable conclusions. We can do this in spite of our emotional subconscious, which may be doing its best to make us believe that black is white, up is down, and bad is beautiful.

As soon as we get into the "why" of our conduct, we're playing in the subconscious' own ballpark: The id, the murky recesses of Freudian theory; the maze of anxieties and frustrations that are the faceless, nameless "monsters" of our nightmares.

We're going to learn how to act and react to the world around us by examining what we do...or don't do...to decide if that's the right way to respond. If it is, we'll reinforce the response. If it isn't, we'll do away with it.

When the subconscious demands to know why we are changing its program, we'll give it the only realistic answer you *can* give to a childish idiot:

"Never mind, you wouldn't understand...and you don't need to know, anyway."

At first, the subconscious will have a fit: It'll try "throwing a tantrum." Soon enough, though, it will learn as any child does that we'll just ignore it...and, like a child, the subconscious will get tired and lose interest quickly.

Failing to monitor our own reaction to life on a continual basis is an open invitation to a listless mental attitude. The subconscious governs to a pervasive extent, running our lives for us, based on its wierd, crazy-quilt programming which began in the womb and has been bombarded by a near infinite variety of unrealistic influences for a lifetime.

There is the story of the young man just discharged from the Navy who decided to have a little fun before settling down. He exhausted first his mustering-out pay and then his parents' patience; sleeping late in the morning, lying around the house most of the day and then prowling the town's night-life each evening.

Finally, his father suggested emphatically that it was time the young man "went out and found a job." Sammy read the want ads; he made the rounds, filling out applications. It wasn't easy as he'd expected. About halfway through the second week he was standing at a bus stop when he heard his name.

"Sammy! —Hey, buddy...what's up?" Turning, he was delighted to see a Navy friend, dressed now in workman's clothes, a lunch bucket in hand.

They exchanged small talk, during which Sammy complained about his difficulty in finding work.

"Well, Sammy," his friend said, "There's an opening where I work: The lathe right next to mine is vacant. The work's not too tough and the pay is alright—it's a job."

"Gee," mused Sammy, "I dunno. I never ran a lathe..."

"Well, you could learn easy enough; I never did before, either. Anyway, you better make up your mind if you're going with me: Here comes our bus."

On the spur of the moment, Sammy climbed aboard the bus with his friend and later that day he was engrossed in learning to operate a lathe in the small machine shop. His immediate problem had been solved.

Twenty-five years later the employees of that shop had a retirement party for Sammy, during the afternoon coffee break. By then he was almost a legend: The oldest employee with the company. His Navy buddy was long-gone; Sammy couldn't even remember his name.

With his plastic coffee cup in one hand and a piece of store-bought cake on a paper plate in his other, Sammy looked around the room at the familiar equipment and the suddenly-strange faces. "Who *are* these people?" Sammy thought. "What the hell! —I'm an old man, now. What happened to all those years? What happened to all those places I never saw; all those things I wanted to do...?"

His eyes glazed and then blurred with tears and as the people and machines faded from view, the noises blended into the background. Suddenly he was seeing a different scene; he heard his name: "Sammy! —Hey, buddy...what's up?" He was young and eager again, standing at a bus stop with his friend. He re-lived the moment of decision, under pressure from an approaching bus, and watched himself shrug and say, "What the hell...why not? What have I got to lose...?"

Someone was tugging at his shop-coat, laughing good-naturedly. "Sammy! Wake up, old man! You wanna spend your life daydreaming?"

Nobody understood the tears running down his face: They thought he was overwhelmed by their farewell gesture.

"Hey, Sammy—You wanna spend your life daydreaming?"

Nobody understood his remark, either: "I just did."

...Sometimes, deciding not to decide anything just yet is the best course of action.

...At *all* times, having a *cognitive awareness* of where we are in life, and where we are heading, is the best course of action.

...Habit is a sedative to thinking; being in a rut is a tranquilizer that glosses over the passage of time.

Nobody said Sammy made a mistake when he decided to get on that bus. He just never questioned, for twenty-five years, whether he should get back off...

Chapter Six

"5---4---3---2---1---Destruct!"

Why do people self-destruct? If doing away with oneself made any sense in the natural (or spiritual) order, why is it that only humans choose to do grave harm to themselves?—And never mind that old slammer about the lemmings: It ain't so; they don't go on suicide marches like people say they do.

The only mass suicide in recent history involved an animal called *homo sapiens;* it took place in a town called Jonesville and sickened the world.

It seems safe to point out that the human animal ranks highest among all known creatures able to experience emotion—feelings. Fat chance a shark would do anything purposely self-destructive! On the other hand, most of us are aware of stories about dogs who reacted to the death of a beloved master by "committing suicide:" They refused to eat or drink. Do dogs have an emotion called grief? They seem to, don't they? Just as they seem able to emote with joy.

It's hardly likely that a dog would commit suicide; but it seems likely that a dog experiencing "terminal grief" simply loses interest in everything around him, including food. In extreme cases, he does, indeed, ultimately die.

Suicide, then, is *not* the product of rational thought. It's ludicrous to try to picture someone arising in the morning and saying, "Hey! Gee, it's a nice day to pull the plug; I think I'll do myself in today!"

People destroy themselves for one reason only: To escape; to get away from or rid of a circumstance that is no longer tolerable. They destroy themselves because of pain.

That's right: Pain. Animals will kill themselves to escape pain; so will humans. The pain can come in either physical or emotional variety; sometimes a mixture of both, and it is pain which, for the individual involved, either exceeds tolerance too much, too long, or too suddenly.

When the pain stems from a physical ailment and there is no hope, no slim chance of recovery, perhaps suicide would even make sense. Terminal cancer victims can use cold logic to arrive at the rational decision that prolonging a life doomed to unimaginable pain and imminent death is *not* intelligent.

Such cases are statistical exceptions. For most of us, the thread of sanity by which we refrain from executing ourselves seems fragile, indeed. Emotional pain—searing, crippling grief, guilt, anxiety—sets the stage for the final act; often the only questions remaining are how...and how soon.

Physical pain, even psychosomatic pain with its roots hidden in the subconscious, is beyond the scope of this work. Pain which can be corrected only by medical science or deep psychiatric probing should, of course, be relieved; but it isn't reasonable to assume that relief can be found or even hidden within these pages.

Emotional pain is our target: Guilt, anxiety, feelings of deep inferiority, grief and remorse are all feelings; they are emotions which cause the sort of pain many people equate with an earnest desire to "end it all." With the exception of grief—some of the time—all of these emotions have a common denominator: We do them to ourselves; they don't "happen to us."

To the conscious mind, in order to "be guilty" you must have done something you, or society, or both, consider a misconduct. The thinking mind can form an accurate conclusion as to whether guilt actually exists.

To the feelings, the emotions, guilt has no bearing

on reality, or vice-versa. People can and do "feel guilty" with little or no concrete, circumstantial reason.

Inferiority is a horse of a similar hue: Ask your conscious mind if you are inferior. Immediately the "computer" will reach for more data: "Inferior—compared to what or whom?" The subconscious, however, has no restrictions placed upon it by simple fact or evidence. It can and does make any conclusion it pleases; based on any data it has (or assumes).

Am I any good? —At what, for Pete's sake...? How can I answer such a general question as that?

—The emotions can answer it, or think they can. Am I any good? Hell, no! —So....what's the sense of keeping up the pretense? Why not just go sit in the car with the engine running and the garage door closed...?

There's a story about a fellow who consulted with a well-known psychiatrist for six months while they tried to get at the source of his deeply-ingrained feelings of inadequacy. At the conclusion of a session, the psychiatrist said, "Mr. J—, I have some good news for you. You need not come for any more sessions: We've established the reason for your inferiority feelings."

"Oh super!" Mr. J— beamed. "What did you find out?"

"You really *are* inferior," the psychiatrist replied.

Have you ever noticed that almost all puns evoke the same reaction: Instead of a chuckle, we groan and make a face? Isn't that because puns are tales woven around a realistic situation, but with a completely incongruous "punch line?" We take the truth and twist it into a "laugh lie." The pun above is no exception. The truth is that many, if not most, suffer from feelings of inadequacy or inferiority. The twist is that a psychiatrist has discovered someone who has genuine reason for his feelings.

Was Mr. J— truly inferior? —compared to what, or whom?

One of the best statements ever made regarding inferiority is this:

You are a child of the universe;
You're not the best,
Or the worst:
You have a right to be here.

Where do we acquire our emotional misinformation that we are guilty, inadequate, inferior? While we come by it in identical ways as a generalization, of course each individual has his or her own peculiar "set" of subconscious programming. We're all alike while all being different, much as grains of sand or snowflakes. A crowd is made up of "people;" isolate any one of those people and you have an individual.

During one counseling session in which a very young (early 20's) wife of two years was trying to come to grips with her anxiety, her destructive feeling of sexual inferiority, she related an incident which took place during the first three months of her marriage:

She came into the living room from the kitchen and, seeing her husband quietly watching TV, she felt a surge of affection for him. He didn't see or hear her approach the chair and was startled when she leaned over and kissed him on the cheek.

He slapped her so violently that she bounced off a wall before falling, almost numb with shock, to the carpet. She'd have been better off if she'd been too numb to hear the words he also clubbed her with:

"Get out of here, you goddamn nymphomaniac!"

When Margaret first began talking to a counselor she was hoping to overcome her growing desire to get away from her husband, her marriage...her grief. She'd been raised to understand, among other things, that sex was dirty and uncomfortable (a wife's duty, nevertheless); and that divorce was simply and absolutely forbidden.

She was virgin when she married: No experience whatsoever with which to program either her conscious or subconscious as to what *she* believed about sex.

Even though her husband was woefully inadequate (but this isn't his story), Margaret found out a fact of life: She *liked* sex —liked it very much.

Margaret is an intelligent, almost brilliant woman; she's simply too young to have acquired enough emotional equilibrium to maintain her balance while she thought the situation through. She did, once, tentatively approach her husband with the suggestion that they talk about the quality of their marriage. Sensing that she might be hinting at separation or divorce, John all 195 pounds of him—lie down on the living room floor like a child and cried disconsolately.

Her mother and her husband were in complete agreement: Sex is sick, it's dirty—and marriages are final. Margaret couldn't reconcile the fact that she really liked sex and did not really like marriage (at least, not what she'd experienced of it).

Her cognitive mind was trying to tell her to run like hell; she was and had been surrounded by sickO's all of her life.

Her subconscious feelings were screaming at her that she was cheap and dirty...guilty...inadequate...or all of the above.

What nearly destroyed Margaret—she had actually stolen enough tranquilizers to kill a horse, from a pharmacy where she worked—was her first two attempts to get help. She'd been to two ministers asking for guidance. All her young life, she'd been told that ministers offer counseling to people who need it. Neither of these men had ever learned how to listen...

Both of them responded with banal platitudes on the nature of marriage and the necessity for "trying." They'd have been more efficient if, instead, they'd offered her a glass of water to wash down the pills. The *last* thing she needed was additional confirmation that there was something wrong with *her.*

What saved Margaret? Actually, it was a shining example of the 180-Degree Theory in operation: With all of her feelings screaming at her that she had no right to live—with the decision already made to kill herself—she did just the opposite. She tried one more time to talk to someone *who would listen*. The world will forever be a little bit brighter place because Margaret lives: She is a truly delightful young woman.

Margaret didn't know about the 180-Degree Theory. She practiced it by accident. Her mother, husband and two ministers had helped her conclude that she had no right to live. When she tried one more time to talk to someone, she no longer questioned her "right to be here" —she had none.

Now, all she wanted was help with one final question. She thought (mistakenly) that she was pregnant. Her young and brutally-scarred ego only wanted help deciding whether to kill herself after the child was born...or take it with her.

Margaret's story could be changed only slightly and would cover a multitude of distressed women whose feelings are twisting their worlds out of shape, making this not a nice place to be. In fact, one counselor once commented that he ought to have some cards printed up, so he could hand one to each woman who came in:

> If you're here because your marriage is driving you nuts—but your husband has no feelings of anything wrong—you can save us both a lot of time and effort: Divorce the bastard.

All of the emotional poisons—the fatal feelings—are to some degree self-administered. There may be an element of reality behind feelings of guilt, inadequacy, inferiority; there frequently is some reality-basis for grief and its first cousin, remorse. When these feelings are strong enough to be deadly, or have been coursing through our psychic veins long enough to build up to critical levels, the poison does its work: It kills us. We are left with only two more decisions: when...and how.

Short of insanity, nobody would make a conscious effort to swallow enough poison, or take sublethal but accruing doses on a regular basis, to cause death. Yet, we do the psychological equivalent of swallowing poison virtually every day. We hand our subconscious—an idiot child—the keys to our psychic pharmacy, and then blindly swallow whatever the idiot child dispenses.

In Margaret's case, she wanted love and sex and the subconscious handed her capsules containing shame, guilt and inferiority. Even during the final days before she truly intended to commit suicide, Margaret's intuition was trying to tell her that she *was not wrong.* When she tried to think things through, she often came up with correct *cognitive* judgments. Her feelings were at war with her cognitive processes, but while she could "feel herself feeling," she could not "hear herself thinking."

Once she *did* hear her rational thought-processes verbalized—because she finally found a listener and was able to think aloud—she discovered that she could take the poison-cabinet keys away from her subconscious. She got well.

Now: Is it a *fact* that sex is dirty?

—Is it a *fact* that marriages must never be terminated, regardless of how terribly one-sided and unfair they may be?

—Is there *anything* wrong with a wholesome, joyful damn-near-abandoned "get it *on!*" attitude toward sex...with your own spouse?

Facts didn't almost destroy Margaret. Feelings did it.

All of the more-or-less self-administered emotional poisons, and even those which "happen to us" such as grief, seem to follow a generalized progression.

First we become victims of feelings of inadequacy or inferiority; we begin to swallow doses of guilt-feelings or we permit grief to gnaw at our emotions. It is at this stage that we can often identify the relationship of the feelings with the real-time,real-life world.

We can understand, by thought-processes, that we are feeling guilty because of a specific act or inaction. We can thoughtfully analyze a job-related or personal relationship failure which generates feelings of inferiority. We can pinpoint the personal loss we suffered which prompted the feelings of grief.

It is at this stage of problem development that we make our tactical error. We tend to shy away from thinking about such situations because to think about them intensifies the emotions involved...and that hurts. We try to get away from the pain; to push it far away from our cognitive mind. "I don't want to think about that..."

What happens? —When the boss computer gives an order, the slave computer follows it. The cognitive mind willfully hands the situation over to the subconscious, conative mind. After that, every time the issue tries to surface into our "thinker," it becomes easier and easier to ignore it until we ultimately have deprived ourselves of the capacity to examine the factual elements; the subconscious is in full control.

The distortion process sets in: The subconscious bends the facts to fit its perceived reality. This may include some genuine information, but it is mostly made up of conditioning from childhood, TV, other people's opinions and a broad assortment of half-lies, outright lies and damned lies.

Below the threshold of our conscious mind the original problem festers. The subconscious simply doesn't know how to handle it; it doesn't want the problem, either, but it has no way to let go of it.

Now the situation which once had some connection, however fragile, to reality, becomes nameless, faceless and formless. Now it has a new name: Anxiety.

And anxiety unrelieved becomes frustration....

Frustration broods its way into depression...

...5...4...3...2...1...Boom!

Self-destructive emotional poison doesn't necessarily end in suicide; although that abruptly final act is the one which gets attention. Suicide is simply the quickest, cheapest and most efficient method of escaping emotional pain. It has only one drawback, but that one is enough to keep most of us from taking this way out: It *will* solve "the problem," but it doesn't really do us much good in the process...

"Emotional suicide" is the agony most of us suffer. It is a self-destructive bent which is neither quick, nor painless, nor inexpensive. It is the subconscious mind's way of avoiding pain. Responding to anxiety, frustration and depression...which hurts...the subconscious frequently leads us to actions which are degrading, painful, self-defeating and even downright destructive.

To a rational mind, trying to cure a problem by causing even bigger problems just doesn't make sense. That's right...and, all along, we've been pointing out that the conative mind is an idiot. To an *idiot*, what makes sense simply will not conform to logic.

What we do, in this condition, is *sublimate:* "Diversion of primitive impulse energy into culturally higher activity." To Margaret's husband John, sublimation of his primal swampland impulses into activity consisted of belting her and calling her a nymphomaniac.

To hundreds—maybe thousands—sublimation of anxiety about sex does, indeed, result in nymphomaniacal activity. Ask almost any family finance counselor what people *usually* do when they suffer anxiety about money and they'll tell you that more often than not, the most marked activity such people become involved in is to go on a credit-buying binge—an illogical, unreasonable frenzy of making their problems worse.

"Culturally higher" activity has a polite-sounding ring to it, doesn't it? Actually, the phrase indicates that the victim has traded a set of feelings (primitive impulses) for an *activity* which can be defined by others.

Ask someone how he feels. If he replies that right at that moment, he feels angry with you—you'd translate his feelings through your own matrix of feelings and logic, and come up with your version of what his primitive impulse was all about.

If, instead of answering you, he employed a culturally higher action such as giving you a black eye, you'd know a whole lot more about how he "feels" toward you.

This sublimation process is emotional suicide: We are destroying ourselves just as surely as if we were to kill ourselves outright. Now, instead of the questions "when" and "how," we might consider our activities as being suicide in progress. Now the questions are "how" and "how long will it take?"

Why do people who know better—who don't genuinely, logically even *want* to:

—Drink excessively...

—Misuse sex frequently...

—Work themselves to death...

—Refuse to work anywhere near their capacity...

—Make war upon people without genuine cause...

—Go through life as "losers"...

Notice...carefully...that even though this list is short, all of these "higher activities" have something in common: None of them are related to reality. None of them have, as inducement for their performance, any semblance of logic. All of them stem from *feelings*... emotions, primitive impulses.

The situational facts in our lives almost never warrant our sublimation, our compensation for the "wrongs" we've done, the inferiorities we have or think we have. Our anxieties are makeshift structures with foundations on quicksand. If we could but employ rational thinking against these actions, these anxieties, we could overcome them and thereby end the self-destruction.

After we've allowed initial problems to become fully internalized, once they've become the property of the unconscious instead of the thinking mind, the downward spiral from higher action to primitive impulse has begun.

We go from a *specific* feeling of guilt, fear, grief, or inferiority, to a non-specific anxiety. Our primitive impulses drive us to action or inaction which is detrimental; we become frustrated (because the sublimation almost never compensates for the anxiety) and depressed.

When something gets fully buried in the mud at the bottom of our subconscious, it's damned hard to dredge it up out without help; either from a professional or a sympathetic and good listener.

The time to prevent the destruction countdown is when we are aware of our feelings; while our thinking self can still discern the nature of the feelings (guilt, grief, shame, etc.)—and can still relate these feelings to the reality-situation which generated them.

What our emotions tell us to do is back away from the feelings because they hurt when we think about them. Here, perhaps more than anywhere else in our lives, we should make *sure* we use the 180-Degree Theory to its utmost. We must all learn to recognize *immediately* the red flag of warning:

"Gosh, I don't want to think about that..."

Remember: Feelings *will* result in action. Handled with our conscious mind in full control, our actions in response to feelings will be governed by situational reality. We can analyze the data, consider the alternatives, and elect the best course of action for all concerned.

Choked back, repressed, our feelings will tailspin downward in our psyche becoming an amorphous mass of primal energy. When the pressure builds sufficiently, these energies will re-surface as action *over which we have no control*; action which is usually unrelated to the situational reality of our lives, and which is usually detrimental to us.

When the subconscious computer gets on the phone to the boss computer and says, "Ouch! Hey, chief...knock it off, will ya? That hurts. I really don't want to think about it..."

That's the time to answer: "Wrong! Sorry to hurt your feelings, idiot, but we are *going* to think about this thing until it's all sorted out. Understand?"

—In other words, just as soon as the feelings stridently urge us to head due north...000 degrees...we put the helm hard over and come about to full south—180 degrees.

Chapter Seven

"A Time Machine Named Desire"

Why do we do some things, and not others? Why some activities with joy; others so reluctantly as to derive only the somewhat perverse satisfaction that we bother with them?

We're talking about motive, aren't we? From junior high school cheerleaders to sales success seminars, from parents to team-mates to spouse and throughout life, someone is always trying to "get us up" to evoke our spirited participation in—something. Anything.

Here's a book over here, purporting to be all we need to make a million dollars in real estate. (It's not that tough, by the way, if you're talking about the *second* million dollars...) Here's another, with a young and foxy lady draped on a chair, legs and arms akimbo (oh, wow!): How to read her like a book (after you buy and read the book she's fronting)... and get anything you want.

Motivation. That's what makes the world spin, isn't it?

Okay; let's start over. Why do we do (or not do) things?

A. Because we want to (don't want to);

B. Because we have to (aren't allowed to).

If we want to go on living, we have to breathe and eat. While eating, we aren't allowed to "swallow" through our windpipes. We can try our best to stay awake indefinitely, but sooner or later the old autonomous "plant maintenance department" is going to over-ride everything and shut down the machinery for repairs and restoration.

All of these do's and don't's are automatic. We have little or no choice in the matter. There is another kind of activity over which we have almost as little control: If we have some compulsion to do or avoid any given activity, it's difficult or impossible to escape the inner urge.

There's still another form of compulsion, one which originates outside of our individual system. That compulsion is called society, for better or for worse. Societies have laws which require certain conduct, or abstentions from other conduct. Even the opposite of society, anarchy, has its compulsions: If the other guy is bigger than you and you have no weapon, you'd best do as he tells you.

On the list of activities of the "want to/don't want to" category, our involvement stems from either a rational decision, or an emotional drive. We may think things through and conclude that something is a good idea; or we may equally as easily go off half-cocked because we *feel* that something is right.

A few years ago, singer Roger Miller recorded a novelty tune, *Chug-a-Lug,* describing the effects of moonshine whiskey. At one point he exhuberantly sings about getting too much alcohol-induced courage and inviting a much larger gentleman "outside" for a round of street boxing. Then, Miller throws in a one-liner that explains both the probable outcome of the event as well as his "reasons" for doing it:

"At the time, it seemed like a good idea..."

Whether our decisionmaker is addled by 99-proof corn whiskey or bamboozled by 99% idiotic subconscious feelings, we often go through life suffering from bruises and abuses—physical and emotional—because we jumped into something just plain dumb... which seemed like a good idea at the time.

We relate to the world around us through *conduct,*

which includes both action and abstention. *All* conduct is preceded by motive, and *all* motive comes under one of two headings:

—We are *required* to do or avoid certain conduct; or

—We *wish* to do or avoid certain conduct.

Somewhere there may be studies which would give statistical evaluations of human conduct. It would be interesting to learn just how much of our conduct stems from *control*, from external compulsion; and then how much after that stems from emotional urge, from feelings—and, finally, how much human conduct is the actual result of deliberate thinking.

Pause for a moment and reflect upon your own situation. How much of your life is genuinely under your control, free from outside pressures? Your license to drive is a contract (one-sided) by which you promise to know and obey traffic laws whenever you use it. You probably used it today to take you to work—still another set of rules and regulations; of things you are required to perform or refrain from.

If you bought a loaf of bread on the way home, you probably paid a tax. The grocer who sold it to you most definitely adheres to a host of laws and codes...or he'd lose his "right" to sell you the bread.

Are you married? There are some laws which govern the relationship you have with your spouse; and there are numerous customs related to this relationship, many of them having almost the force of law.

So: How much self-control is left to you? Fifty percent? If you were awake fourteen hours today, did you have a cumulative total of seven hours in which you could "do as you pleased?"

Now think about the events of the day which evoked an emotional response: How many decisions, large and small, were based on the immediate urge of your emotions, your feelings? How frequently did you have the solid, thoughtful or intuitive sense that your decision was absolutely right and proper for the conditions at hand?

There aren't any pat answers. It is fairly apparent,

though, that most of us are directed by outside forces most of the time. We seldom realize it, because we are card-carrying members of the society that makes the rules; we are conforming largely through choice and so it seems as though we are doing what we want to do.

For the remaining portion of our life, wherein our conduct is discretionary, most of us seem to be guided by feelings most of the time. Of the precious minutes remaining, much of that is disposed of by habit—we're in a rut—and on rare occasions, we actually decide by thinking what our specific conduct-response will be in a specific set of circumstances.

Habit isn't necessarily bad. By establishing a set pattern of reaction to some circumstances we can relegate the effort of thinking to the subconscious mind. We don't have to pay any particular attention to what we're doing when we are operating on "automatic pilot."

The problem with this is that habit is all pretty much alike in the sense of achievement or reward. It's too bad, for instance, that kissing your wife can become such a habit-routine that it packs all the emotional whallop of picking your nose...

Someone once defined a "rut" as a grave that's still open on two ends. Being "in a rut," functioning largely from habit, relieves us of having to use our mind—but we pay an exhorbitant price for this convenience: Life itself becomes a muted shade of gray, flavorless and listless.

A moment ago we mentioned kissing your wife (husband, mate) as a matter of habit. Can you remember the last time you kissed like that, out of habit? Can you *really* remember it, or are you just certain that it happened because it always happens at a certain time or place?

Now...can you remember the *very first time* you two kissed each other? —You bet you can! Which did you prefer...?

We have all traded a huge percentage of our right to be self-determining in exchange for the security provided by law and custom. We are members of society and society itself would come unglued if all of us didn't trade our decision-rights for the overall rights of our fellow citizens.

Next, we have all *given away* a significant percentage of our self-determination by allowing ourselves to be swallowed up by a rut. We've put bits in the mouth of imagination and handed the reins to our idiot subconscious. "Here, you drive," we've said; "you lead, I'll follow."

It's only a small step from allowing habit to direct us to giving emotional feelings the helm. Now when confronted by circumstances which habit alone can't handle, we're guided by our feelings. Either way, we don't have to do much thinking and, somehow, we seem to muddle through.

Have you ever noticed how strange it seems when you are faced with a situation which *demands* that you *think* about it? How familiar is the thought, "ohmigod, what'll I do now?" Do you roll your eyes from side to side, vainly looking for the answer that always "seems to be there" when your automatic responses are functioning?

"Harvey, both of the kids need new shoes." (fact)

"Maude, we just can't afford it." (habitual reaction)

"Well, that's too damn bad. What shall I do, keep 'em home from school until you think we can afford it?" (emotion)

"Maude, will you lighten up on me?" (emotional reaction)

"Harvey, they're *your* kids, too!" (another fact)

—Now Harvey will think about the situation, analyzing all the data available to him. Once he does this, the answer seems fairly clear. He asks one more question:

"Can either one of them make do for one more week, Maude?"

"Well," she relents, "Jimmy could use his sneakers."

"Then," Harvey decides, "Well buy Lisa some

shoes this payday; and Jimmy gets his next payday. Okay?"

"Yeah, sure, Harv. More coffee?"

Of the four kinds of motivation, we seem to use least the one which is most clearly under our rational control; and we are most influenced by motivation we have little to do with.

The four motivators are:

1. External compulsion (law, society, customs).
2. Internal compulsion (subconscious drives).
3. Feelings (subconscious urges, habits).
4. Rational decisions (cognitive processes).

Our personal ability to control these is in reverse order. We can control:

1. *All* cognitive processes.
2. *Most* feelings.
3. *Some* psychological compulsions.
4. *Few* external directions.

One of the perversities of human nature is illustrated by the fact that thousands of men will do some in-depth thinking about which baseball team will win the pennant (which the individual can do absolutely nothing about); and virtually *no* thinking about improving the quality of his own life (which he could do a great deal about if he'd revoke the idiot subconscious' license to "drive").

Using the 180-Degree Theory, we are gong to discover how to resume control of our own individual destiny. We're going to learn how to stop running in reverse, being pushed about by circumstance and habit and emotions. It will take some genuine effort and some time, but it will work.

First, however: You have to decide (with your *head*, not your feelings) how badly you want to recover the right to paddle your own canoe. As the comedian George Carlin puts it, "you gotta wanna."

—You don't have to improve yourself.

—You're under no deep, compulsive drive to become mentally self-sufficient.

—You may not even feel "good" about doing it.

—But you *can* decide that you *want* to. That decision, wanting to, is the first step. Once you generate the wilful, thoughtful desire, you'll have created a time machine which will take you to a better lifestyle at an ever-increasing pace.

It becomes your personal time machine named Desire.

Chapter Eight

"If They Only Knew"

Most of us spend much of our time hiding from other people. We do our jobs, attend meetings of our chosen organizations, go to parties—and always we make an effort to "be better" than we secretly believe we really are.

One counselor friend of the authors told us that he never considers a new client to be making any progress until he hears, at one of the sessions, some variation on the comment,

"If you only knew what I'm really like inside, you'd probably give up on me."

This predisposition to self-censure seems to be at least a national characteristic; if not part of the organized human race itself.

We watch those around us and privately we wonder how they are able to function to effortlessly, so un-self consciously, when we are usually so miserably aware of ourselves in a social setting. What we are seeing, and misrepresenting to ourselves as self-confidence in others, is the false face they are wearing. Sure, they're hiding too...we all do it.

Several times daily we're asked, casually, "How are you?" Dr. Bob enjoys answering this habitual question with a resounding, "Super!"

Invariably, his response gets attention. The word "super" isn't fair...the question was only habit, anyway; and the expected answer is something like: "Oh, okay I guess..."

To reply that you are at peace with the world and enjoying life, to show any sign of exuberance, only reminds the other person that there *are* degrees of "how we are" —that "okay, I guess" is dull grey and two-dimensional in a world full of color and dimension.

And yet, close associates of Dr. Bob would be unable to count the number of times he has confided in them about some personal difficulty—prefaced by the signal-phrase, "If people only knew..."

Two observations about our hidden shortcomings:

—People *do* know. That quirk you anxiously hide from everybody...? —If they know you at all well, they probably are as fimiliar as you are with the idiosyncracy. Does it "bother" them? Why should it...it's yours, not theirs.

—The "shortcoming" looms much bigger than life in your mind; to anyone else it would rate a minor shrug of the shoulder.

Once a young married woman on a hospital staff stopped at the psychologist's office and said, "I think I'd better make an appointment with you. There's something I probably ought to talk to you about."

"Sure, Nancy," he said. "Is it something that'll keep, or should we try to get to it right away? How much does it seem to pick at you?"

"Well..." —Watching her reaction, he was aware that she wanted to get it out in the open soon; but that she was probably not in deep, immediate trouble. In other words, she simply was having a hard time "keeping it inside" but a full discussion could wait a while.

Casually, he asked her, "Was it good, Nance?"

She blushed, then smiled and replied, "You betcha!"

"How about Thursday at two o'clock?" He asked.

"...See you then," she replied, and went about her job.

Later, during the conversation, Nancy described how her marriage was all over but the formalities, and how she had become involved with another man whom she very probably would marry. She'd had what amounted to an extramarital affair—her first and only—and was in love.

The love, and the marriage intention, seemed to make it okay in her mind. However, the tabu against such conduct which had been programmed into her subconscious began eating at her peace of mind.

As she went about her routine duties, she kept thinking that if her acquaintances only knew the truth about her, they would probably condemn her. Part of her wanted to tell the world; the other part wanted to hide. She was in conflict and she knew it; as she passed the psychologist's office that morning something "clicked" and, on the spur of the moment, she decided to get it off her chest.

Everybody who knew her at all well during those few days probably was aware that "something's wrong with Nance;" although they wouldn't have been concerned enough to try to figure it out.

In the setting of talking to a psychologist about something that was bothing her; and because of the nature of his profession and considering the odds, the man was able to make an accurate "stab in the dark" that hit the target.

The part we all hide from others (or think we do) is the part, or parts, we think of as our "if only's". If only "they" knew I never have the courage to stand my ground...If only "they" knew I'm only making $4.50 an hour...If only "they" knew how it scares me to make a cold sales call...

What would happen if "they found out?" Would we be led through the city gates and stoned to death if "they" discovered our secret faults? *Why* do we hide?

Perhaps more importantly: What price do we pay for our secrets, our evasions?

The price we pay is that we set arbitrary and usually unfair limits upon what we expect from life. Because we are using a personal merit system to establish how "good" or "bad" we are in our own estimation, it inexorably follows that we will use that same scale to determine what we *deserve* from life.

How do you honestly (secretly) rate yourself as a husband or wife? Okay...how satisfactory a marriage do you then "deserve?"

If your employer ever found out about your "if only's" on the job—if he only knew about your secret shortcomings—how would it affect your income? If you were suddenly to be paid based absolutely on "what you deserve," would you get a raise in pay—or a pay cut?

It is a strange thing, but very true: We go through our whole lifetime making value judgements about what we deserve, and those judgments play a major role in our conduct.

Pay careful attention: *Nobody is born deserving anything,* either bad or good. We are going to examine a verbatim quote from the *New Oxford Dictionary* to see what "deserve" is all about:

> DESERVE: (1) Be entitled by conduct or qualities to (reward or treatment; to be or to do); (2) Have established a claim to be well or ill treated at the hands of...

In order to *deserve* (anything), we must have become entitled to it by *conduct;* or because we possess certain *qualities.* We are required to *establish a claim* upon the way others treat us—whether well or ill treatment—before we can *deserve* treatment of any sort.

Nowhere is there some gigantic, cosmic lottery wheel which pre-determines *who* deserves *what* in this game called life. The U.S. Declaration of Independence says it succinctly:

"...all (wo)men are created equal..."

Make no mistake about the meaning of that. We begin as equals, much like horses lined up in a racetrack starting gate. The moment we are born, life hollers: "Get ready...get set...GO!" From then on, life is a competition. When those racehorses lined up, which of them deserved to win—or lose? Only one of them will *establish a claim* to the winner's wreath: The horse first across the finish line *deserves* to win.

What if the jockey of one of those horses decided, for whatever reason, that his horse "didn't deserve" victory? The jockey could keep the horse from running first. Would that mean that the horse actually deserved to win (but didn't); or that it didn't deserve to lose (but did)?

—What it would really mean is that the horse *didn't deserve* the treatment it received from the jockey. What right did he have to decide *what* the horse deserved? Only winning or losing can establish the deserved outcome of a race. When an outside interference or influence artifically changes—inhibits—natural abilities, the final outcome is going to be something unfair.

Your subconscious is the jockey on your back!

What do you deserve from life? There's only one way to establish that: Find out what you can achieve from life when you give it your best shot. Don't let your subconscious-jockey decide what you deserve before you start the race...

Because I failed at a marriage...failed at several attempts to start small businesses...failed to achieve fame and fortune...am I a failure? *IS that what I deserve?* My subconscious says it is. If there's one thing my subconscious understands very well, it's how to do it wrong; to fail. And if there's one thing my idiot subconscious *can't* understand, it is simply this: *The race isn't over, yet!*

Every time I feel that pulling back on the reins because my subconscious "feels"' I'm striving for something I don't deserve, it's time for the 180-Degree Theory: Take the bit in clenched teeth and go flat-out toward the finish line. In this situation, you might want to tell your subconscious-jockey, "Hang on and pay attention, Dummy...you know how to ride a loser; we're going to teach you how to ride a winner."

Perhaps word-pictures about jockies and races

won't give some readers the full perspective of the life-importance of this ego-trip we call "deserve." For another view, let's go back and visit General Custer's ghost one last time. Earlier, we promised to share a little-known fact that might shed some light on Custer's illogical action.

This is "iffy," because we don't (and never will) have all the background that goes along with the facts. However, let's make some suppositions.

Let's suppose that Custer, like all of the rest of us, was hiding some insecurities. Let's suppose he, for reasons known only to him, allowed his subconscious to persuade him that "if other people only knew the truth", he'd be found out and ridiculed as a career military officer.

Since this is our supposition, we can carry it one step further and suppose that he was past anxiety and frustration and had become depressed—that he was emotionally suicidal.

History nowhere questions Custer's courage, so it's not likely that he would have *decided* to commit suicide...at least not with his cognitive mind.

What history *does* question is why General Custer, shortly before the ill-fated cavalry march to the Little Big Horn, talked several of his officers into buying life insurance...Custer and a number of his staff purchased insurance policies of several thousand dollars each; 100 years ago these were large policies. Even then, the U.S. Army had provisions for caring for wives and families of officers killed in the line of duty. Why did Custer decide to encourage these men to buy additional protection...? Why did he feel it was a good idea for himself...?

Remember the definition of sublimation; our subconscious mind's way of upgrading undefined primitive urges into definable action—not always in our genuine best interest. Is it reasonable to suppose that Custer had no genuine, logical reason for wanting more insurance? Certainly it would be difficult to think of rational motive for persuading many of his staff officers to imitate his action.

It isn't unreasonable to conjecture that Custer's unconscious psyche had decided that he "didn't deserve to continue." Somewhere in the mish-mash between cognition and conative input it was also decided that his survivors "didn't deserve" the financial loss. By extension, neither did the survivors of anyone who accidentally got in the way if and when Custer's primitive energy impulses erupted in "culturally higher activity"; the sublimation intented to remove completely all of his anxiety sources.

All of that, of course, is conjecture. The only facts we have are these: Custer bought a major life insurance policy and convinced a number of his officers to do likewise. Soon thereafter, this man who knew better took those officers and 200-plus enlisted men into action against an enemy force known to outnumber them more than 20 to 1.

Was he on an ego trip? Did he thoughtfully decide that he was such a superior general that the odds didn't matter? Was it the "Peter Principle"—had the Army promoted a good colonel into a rank one step above his level of competence, creating a mediocre general?

Was it simple stupidity?

—Or was it motivation from "the jockey on his back," a subconscious which had decided he didn't deserve to win?

Let's visit that dusty army post and listen as the troop responds to the bugler's call to boots and saddles:

"Hey, Corporal—Where we goin'?" asks a hung-over private.

"Little Big Horn," the corporal replies grimly.

"What?!" the private can't believe he heard right. "I was drinking with that scout Crazy Fox last night. Cripes, he says there's thousands of injuns at the Horn—and with Geronimo there, too!"

"I know it." The corporal isn't talkative.

"Well, what's the matter with Custer? Is he nuts? He could get us all killed!"

"Soldier," the corporal says as he throws a knee into his horse, tightening the cinch, "I'll pretend I didn't hear what you just said about the General. Now: Saddle that damn horse!"

—Orders, as Willie once told Joe as they slogged through Italy, "is orders."

The private was heard to mutter one last thing as he swung into the saddle: "Man, this is suicide!"

—Was he right? Was it suicide; one man's sub-ego deciding that performance of the pending military action would result in what Custer "deserved?"

We'll never know. But the lesson drawn from this should be clear to us all: Whether Custer deserved his fate at the hands of those Indians is a question that pales to insignificance at the next one: Did 250 men and officers deserve to go with him, if it was emotionally-inspired "suicide?"

We must all stop allowing our subconscious to shape the outlines of what we deserve. How you or I *feel* about what we deserve has no bearing on what others think we deserve. And *only when others perceive our actions is this issue resolved.* In order to truly establish any *claim* we have to put points on the scoreboard. We don't deserve to win just because we want to very, very much. Neither do we deserve to lose because our subconscious "feels" we're not good enough to be a winner.

The multi-million-dollar Arbuckle's Coffee fortune was made on the slogan, "You get what you pay for." By extension, you get paid for what you do—or don't do. We all start even in the gate: Nobody anywhere has any method of determining which of us deserves anything, good or bad, before the race is begun.

We are not considering only fame and fortune, either. Which of us deserves *gemutlichkeit:* The expansive sense of wellbeing that comes only to those at peace with the world around them? Unfortunately, huge numbers of us today have concluded we don't deserve happiness. *Who says so?* The simple but somehow amazing truth is that there isn't anyone anywhere whose responsibility is deciding who will be happy and who will not. You can't apply for a license or permit to happiness: There's no place to make such an application.

Every American citizen is guaranteed the right to—not happiness—but to the *pursuit* of happiness. The same sentence in the founding declaration of this nation says we all *begin equal*; and we all have a *right to try* to be(come) happy.

Your subconscious...my subconscious...everyone's "feelings" from time to time will attempt to repeal the U.S. Declaration of Independence and the Bill of Rights as it applies to us personally.

"What others don't know about me" is the secret knowledge I carry around, locked up in my psyche, which causes me to hide from others. I (if I listen to my subconscious) will try to prevent others from making me "pay" for my shortcomings—I *don't* want what my feelings tell me I actually "deserve."

Nobody asked to be born, right?

(*You are a child of the Universe.*)

We all have shortcomings, we're all guilty of some misconduct, we all have had reason for some amount of shame.

(*You're not the best...*)

However, not many of us *want* to be evil; few of us actually could be considered shameful.

(*...or the worst...*)

Maybe we should all take another look at what we "deserve," starting with one bench-mark we can use as a foundation:

(*You have a right to be here.*)

Many will be familiar with the popular Sunday newspaper supplement, the "comics section," and the cartoon character Pogo: Both Pogo and Puck, who heralds the Sunday funnies, use a slightly-amended version of a famous military quotation to make a basic observation about life:

"We have met the enemy and he is us."

The incessant friction between our cognitive mind

and our conative feelings—the tug between what we *think* we want from life and what we *feel* we deserve—is an internal civil war. Nobody around us knows the war is being waged; they are all too busy waging wars of their own.

Look around you in a public place: Look for the chewing of lips, the furrowed brow, the deep sigh...when the person is talking to *nobody*—except himself, his feelings. Later in this book we are going to become deeply involved in trying to understand where we are *now*; and where we want to go in life. Be careful!

So many of us make the mistake of discovering a deep, intuitive insight about what we want for the future, and then "give away" the present trying to make a quantum leap toward that attainable but distant life-style.

LIFE IS WHAT HAPPENS TO YOU WHILE YOU ARE PLANNING FOR THE FUTURE...The 180-Degree Theory is a vehicle we use for a *journey*; it is a time machine, not an instant remedy. We must learn to be on guard for the struggle between cognition and conative processes which will result when we begin earnestly trying to *become* something.

As long as you can sincerely and intelligently *think things through* on matters of what you intend to achieve from life; and how you intend to achieve these things, you must learn to deal with the "backfire" from your *feelings*. You will be misinformed, by feelings; either that you "don't deserve" something you want and have an intelligent right to seek after, or that you "deserve" some form of failure.

The importance of learning to reconcile thought and emotion as to the individual "deservings" of each and every one of us is summed up in this quote from Joshua Loth Liebman, author of *Peace of Mind:*

> Social peace can never be permanently achieved so long as individuals engage in civil war with themselves. Peace of mind is the gift God reserves

for his special proteges. *Talent* and beauty He gives to many. Wealth is commonplace. *Fame* not rare. But Peace of Mind is His final merit of approval, the fondest sign of His love. I know now that the sum of all other possessions does not necessarily add up to peace of mind; yet, on the other hand, I have seen this inner tranquility fluorish without the material supports of property or even the blessings of physical health. Peace of Mind is not something that can be bought in bottles, or applied like a cosmetic to the surface of the skin.

When you are striving to become all you can be, you are pitting the best you have against the worst the world can throw at you. It is this contest which *determines* what you deserve. It won't always seem "fair," but in the long run; in the final analysis, the outcome depends more upon you than upon anything else.

Luck can enter the picture, both good and bad. We can learn to accept the good gratefully and hopefully accept the bad: Not as an omen, a sign that we're "getting what we have coming to us," but simply as an element of the contest which is as unpredictable as the weather...or good luck.

Starting now, make it crystal clear to your subconscious feelings that you will not ever again be swayed by any emotional judgments or prejudices about your "rights."

You have a right to be here.

You have a right to life, liberty and the pursuit of happiness.

You have the right to become all you *can* be.

Don't allow an internal civil war to destroy your peace of mind while you are enroute to your future.

When your subconscious mind trys to tell you that you will get what you deserve, remind it of the 180-Degree Theory:

"No, I'm not going to 'get what I deserve,' I'm going to *deserve whatever I get.*"

Chapter Nine

"Act Your Way to a New Feeling"

In his Earlier publication, *Feelings,* Dr. Bob suggested that, "It's a lot easier to act your way to a new feeling than it is to feel your way to a new action." Amen!

Feelings are those tricky, emotional, immature sensations urging us to perform actions; sometimes vaguely-defined and *always* poorly thought through. Actions come in two varieties: There is the kind of action which stems from *cognition*—things we do because our brain wants to. And then there is the kind of action called *sublimation.* You'll recall that this kind is the result of primitive urge-energy surfacing through wayward activity—usually if not always detrimental to us.

If we continue to permit ourselves to feel our way to a new action, it will usually be this primitive urge/act syndrome which governs our lives to an unacceptable degree. Planning becomes a mockery, because planning is a function of our rational mind and the subconscious can (and does) ignore much of what goes on in our "head."

People who feel their way to new action—most of us who never knew we have a choice—are victims of this little two-act play:

Act One: "Boy, I'm *never* gonna do *that* again!"

Act Two: "Now...*why* did I *do* that again...?"

Nobody will ever completely free him or herself

from the kind of sublimated action our subconscious serves up. The 180-Degree Theory is a method of improving the odds; a way to elevate our win/loss percentage above .500 into the winner's circle more often than not. So long as we *have* emotions and a subconscious we are going to have periods of anxiousness and moments of anxiety. Anxiety is going to continue to make us do the strangest things...things we wouldn't do if we were computers or creatures without feelings.

However, every one of us *can* make an effort to perform actions we *want* to perform; actions we've carefully considered and decided are in our best interest. The subconscious mind learns from our conscious mind all the time, it is infinitely re-programmable; *and it believes whatever we tell it.*

This is the reason why numerous self-help "isms" work at least some of the time. We learn from various cult leaders or self-improvement gurus how to concentrate on certain aspects of our personality; and the repetitive message will indeed re-program the subconscious.

Many of us are aware of "techniques" which instruct us to tape messages to ourselves on the mirror at home where we'll see them several times a day. "I will become a better salesman," they say; or "I am going to be successful today." There is one common method which has us going about repeating the phrase, "Every day in every way I'm getting better and better."

These techniques are partially successful because they are based on the demonstrated fact that we can retrain our subconscious: It will indeed believe what we tell it.

And these techniques are partially unsuccessful because they don't allow for individual personality styles. If all of us taped the following message on the mirror, it would work for some of us and not for others. In fact, it might prove to be detrimental to some of us. The message:

"Today I am going to be outgoing, exciting. I will

sparkle!"

To the *sensitives* and *outspokens,* this would be duck soup: Their natural inclination is to be this way , anyway; the reinforcement would add to a natural personality trait.

To the *pushers* and *examiners* this would be much more difficult. Those of us whose personalities do not contain the "spark" of expressiveness are forced to "fake it." And, of course, that's how we come off: Fakes.

Now: Supposing your subconscious is already loaded with self-dislike because you're not a more colorful person. You've just read a book on how to become the life of the whatever, and your first assignment was to tape the above message on your mirror and go to the office the next morning and "knock 'em over" with your "new" personality.

Your conscious mind, having thought about what you've read, is ready to make the shift from quiet and reserved to outspoken and scintillating—in one day, no less. The unconscious...the feelings...are in agreement, because your feelings have been pestering you for a long time to be more like a superstar.

Of course, you bomb in your new act. You don't know *how* to be the life of the party/office/car pool: Being expressive takes *practice,* like everything else we do. The entire process of taking the conversational and personality leadership role is new and awkward to you. You have the sensation that you are trying to tiptoe through a roomful of marbles, wearing unlaced combat boots.

Elaine comes to work and asks, "Hey: How do you like my new hair color?" The genuine outspoken immediately comes back with, "What'd you do—spill ink on it?" —and everybody laughs. So, following your instructions to be more "with it," you immediately add: "Yeah...you're supposed to put shoe polish on your *shoes*, Elaine!" —And everything suddenly goes quiet. You'd swear you can hear your watch ticking. The silence lasts for an eternity, during which you realize that you've just offended Elaine. She's hurt.

After this and maybe a few more similar experiences, your cognitive mind concludes that there's something wrong with you because the self-help program just doesn't work. In fact, it frequently backfires. Your subconscious mind is chasing its emotional tail and chanting, "Told you so...told you so...you're no good...you're no good..."

What you've just done is try to ram a square peg into a round hole: You've mangled both the edges of the square peg and the smooth contours of the round hole. You got hurt; so did others around you because you were out of character. In the little story above, Elaine has worked with you for three years and has unconsciously come to depend upon you (an examiner) for quiet thoughtfulness and precise, well-articulated opinions. Last Monday you told her she looked like she'd shampooed with Shinola.

If she "expected" anything from you during that little episode, it was for you to approach her later in the day when nobody else was nearby and reassure her; or even make a slightly critical suggestion. Either:

"Elaine, your hair is pretty that color," or:

"Elaine, you've got the right idea: Your hair is pretty like that. I wonder if more red highlights, next time, wouldn't make it even nicer..."

A pusher or an examiner will never comfortably make the switch to being bubbly and back-slapping. The outspoken and to a slightly-lessened degree the sensitive will never be able to become thoughtful, reserved and quiet. And, as we've mentioned several times and will keep mentioning, *there is no one better* "way to be" than the others. The best way for *you*...the *only* way that makes sense for you...is *what you are.*

If you know a pusher, a usually-quiet and unexpressive individual who is a little bit autocratic and demanding, get a mental image of this person solidly placed in your mind's eye. Now: Imagine this same individual suddenly trying to be very warm towards everyone around him or her. He or she goes from one to another, asking how they feel today; if they are happy with their job, or asking about their families.

Of course, the image is incongruous. The typical reaction to this would be, "I wonder what he wants from me...?"

However, if a sensitive approached you and seriously asked how your kids are doing in school, you'd think nothing of it—other than a "feeling" that the person cared about you and was interested in you.

If an examiner came roaring into the salesroom wearing loud clothes and making extravagent gestures while talking a mile-a-minute about breaking sales records today...his fellow salesmen would leap to the conclusion that he'd come to work drunk. Harry—who *is* an outspoken—came in the same way five minutes earlier...and nobody noticed. Had Harry come into the room quietly, looking thoughtful and subdued, his fellow workers would assume *he* was suffering from a hangover.

A nationally-famous comedian has created a fictional character whose well known one-liner always brings a big chuckle:

"Honey, what you *see* is what you *get!*"

How true this is, when we are dealing with personality types. What we *are* usually shows in our attitudes, our actions, our clothing, our demeanor—in a thousand and one little small ways that others unconsciously "pick up" when they are dealing with us in life. Any attempt to artificially be something we are not simply makes others confused and uncomfortable; and it seems to make us even more unsure of ourselves when it doesn't work out the way we planned it.

The concept of "acting your way to a new feeling" *will* work, if the changes we are trying to bring about fit into our overall personality style. The chances of making any beneficial change, any lasting change, which is contrary to our normal personality, are not likely to satisfy either rationally or subconsciously.

A salesperson can use these techniques to become a better salesperson, as long as he or she understands exactly what personal assets are to be reinforced and used to full advantage. Where people often fail is to assume that they will become better salespeople after they've "improved their personalities." They don't know any more about selling than they did before; they have no new contacts and no really effective approach that wasn't there yesterday. Now the only difference is that they make prospects uncomfortable because they are operating contrary to what they really are.

The subconscious can make us truly afraid of approaching people of wealth and status: We "freeze up" when we try to sell them something. The answer is *not* to become an outspoken, flashy individual (unless you are already); it is, instead, to use the "act your way to a new feeling" technique to overcome being needlessly intimidated by another's social status.

To employ this technique, we need first to understand the relationship of the subconscious and the cognitive mind, as discussed in detail earlier in this book. The subconscious is a slave-computer, a servomechanism without any well defined capability to think. It is our "feelings factory," the source of emotion and autonomous plant maintenance. It derives its programming from external sources (TV, our environment, our formative years) and from our *cognitive* mind—our thinker.

The subconscious *cannot* discern truth or falsity. It will believe anything that happens to lodge in its memory. Because of this, we can utterly convince the subconscious that something about us is defective. Earlier, we mentioned a beautiful woman whose life has been detrimentally affected because she has convinced her subconscious she has an ugly nose. There are people who are terrified of meeting strangers in a social setting because they "aren't interesting" to others. The list has no end: Fill in your own personal "quirks."

The key to these things is that we can identify, with our intelligence, those things which simply are not *facts* but which the subconscious accepts as unvarnished truth. And we can also identify things about us which are *not* true—but which we'd like to be true—and simply lie to the subconscious. Why not...it will believe bad things about us which aren't true; why shouldn't we fill it full of good things that are equally untrue *today.*

Just as the subconscious causes us to perform actions which are appropriate for the incorrect image it has formed now; it is equally capable of helping us perform actions in keeping with the *new* image we want it to have.

We do this by *acting.* We reverse the communication between conscious and unconscious. Rather than continuing to perform the same actions over and over again because we are subconsciously programmed to do it that way, we do it the way we *want* to...even though it feels awkward at first...and this changes the program.

The unconscious plays a terribly important role in how we act and react in life. If I have a very unflattering self-image, even though there is no genuine reason to "feel" inferior, I will *act* inferior in hundreds of small ways I am not aware of.

As I walk into a restaurant, for example, I'll shuffle; my eyes will be downcast. If someone is standing partially in the way, I'll mumble something apologetic as I slide past. My hair will be out of place, my clothing less than attractive. The *subconscious* tells my muscles how to walk, to talk, to handle my tableware. It can even produce a whopping "mental block" when the waitress asks what I'd like—I'm liable to apologize for taking her time.

It doesn't take many times of walking into a restaurant 180-Degrees differently before my subconscious learns how to do that, also; and equally as well. Head up, shoulders back; don't shuffle, dammit! —stride. Someone partly in the way? —They'll see me coming. They'll move: Why not, it's a passageway, not a standing-way. Hair out of place? No way: I combed it before I got out of the car; just before I checked to see if the shirt was tucked in and the socks pulled up...

In other words, I acted like *I am sombody* when entering the restaurant. Before long, the subconscious does all of this as automatically as it did the wrong things before.

In other words: I acted like a nobody because that was how my feelings pictured me; then I reversed the process and acted like a sombody, causing my feelings to believe that, instead.

My feelings make me act like a nobody.

My actions make me feel like a somebody.

When we practice living on a rational basis as opposed to allowing the feelings to guide us, acting our way to a new feeling becomes an integral part of our lifestyle. We may at first find ourselves exerting conscious effort to perform new actions/activities...but with surprising speed, the subconscious "learns this new game"' to the extent that we do this re-programming almost constantly with little attention.

Apparently, the subconscious is more comfortable when the conscious is in charge most of the time. It seems that to the majority of us, an inversion of this relationship has caused the unconscious to operate out of its element. What we are doing is restoring the proper relationship; after which the twin-computer set-up seems to function more efficiently.

It should. It was "designed" that way, and we've been steering a course 180 degrees out of line. We've been living with a system whereby feelings cause actions which reinforce the feelings; we're going to trade that for a system wherein actions change feelings for the better, *then* reinforce them.

Chapter Ten

"Please Hear What I'm NOT Saying"

How well do you listen? Do people seem to seek you out, to confide in you and ask for your reactions? All of us know at least a few people who seem to be more understanding than others. We are unfortunate, indeed, if there isn't at least one person among our acquaintances who will act as a "sounding board" for our thoughts and ideas.

Such people have a reputation for giving sound advice. Perhaps they've earned this reputation, but the odds are that they do little in the way of advising. It's far more likely that they are *good listeners.*

A good listener gives us the opportunity to verbalize our plans or problems. We hear ourselves enumerating the alternatives; defining the circumstances and conditions. As we do this, the proper course of action seems to surface and our friend simply reinforces our newly-formed conclusions.

Remember: A friend is someone who leaves you with all of your freedoms intact, but obliges you to be fully what you are...or to become fully all you can be.

One of our most elementary freedoms—and the responsibility that goes with it—is to chart our own course in life; to be in charge of our own personal destiny. The freedom and responsibility to make our own decisons often finds us in a quandry. When the confusion becomes untenable, we seek out a friend for advice. If he or she is a real friend, we will be left free to decide—but obligated to decide well, to our true best interests. A good friend does this far better by listening than by "telling."

There is a magnificent, poetic work—author unknown—which underlines the deep need each of us has for someone else who will listen. It also hints at the enormous value each of us can achieve by *becoming* good listeners.

Please Hear What I'm NOT Saying

Don't be fooled by me.
    Don't be fooled by the face I wear.
For I wear a mask, I wear a thousand masks,
    masks that I'm afraid to take off,
    and none of them are me.
Pretending is an art that's second nature with me,
    but don't be fooled, for God's sake don't be fooled.
I give you the impression that I'm secure,
    that all is sunny and unruffled with me,
    within as well as without,
    that confidence is my name and coolness is my game,
    that the water's calm and I'm in command,
    and that I need no one.
But don't believe me.
Please.
My surface may seem smooth, but my surface is my mask,
    my ever-varying and ever-concealing mask.
Beneath lies no smugness, no complacence.
Beneath dwells the real me in confusion, in fear,
    in aloneness.
But I hide this.
I don't want anybody to know it.
I panic at the thought of my weakness and fear being exposed.
That's why I frantically create a mask to hide behind,
    a nonchalant, sophisticated facade,
    to help me pretend,
    to shield me from the glance that knows.

But such a glance is precisely my salvation,
    my only salvation.
And I know it.
That is...if it is followed by acceptance,
    if it's followed by love.
It's the only thing that can liberate me, from myself,
    from my own self-built prison walls,
    from the barriers that I so painstakingly erect.
It's the only thing that will assure me of what I can't
    assure myself,
    that I'm really worth something.
But I don't tell you this,
    I don't dare.
    I'm afraid to.
I'm afraid your glance will not be followed by
    acceptance
and love.
I'm afraid that you will think less of me,
    that you'll laugh,
    and your laugh would kill me.
I'm afraid that deep down I'm nothing,
    that I'm just no good,
    and that you will see this and reject me.
So I play my game, my desperate pretending game,
    with a facade of assurance without,
    and a trembling child within.
And so begins the parade of masks.
And my life becomes a front.
I idly chatter to you in the suave tones of surface talk.
I tell you everything that really nothing...
    ...and nothing of what's everything,
    of what's crying within me.
So when I'm going through my routine do not be fooled
    by what I'm saying.
Please listen carefully and try to hear
    what I'm *not* saying,
    what I'd like to be able to say,
    what for survival I *need* to say,
    but what I *can't* say.
I dislike hiding. Honestly.

I dislike the superficial game I'm playing,
the superficial, phony game.
I really like to be genuine and spontaneous...
...and me...
but you've got to help me.
You alone can break down the wall behind which I tremble.
You alone can remove my mask,
you alone can release me from my shadow-world of panic and uncertainty,
from my lonely prison.
So do not pass me by. Please do not pass me by.
It will not be easy for you.
A long conviction of worthlessness builds strong walls.
The nearer you approach to me, the blinder I may strike back at you.
It's irrational, but despite what the books say about man,
I am irrational.
I fight against the very thing that I cry out for.
But I am told that love is stronger than strong walls,
and in this lies my hope.
My only hope.
Please try to beat down those walls with firm hands,
but with gentle hands...
for a child is very sensitive.
Who am I, you may wonder: I am someone you know very well.
For I am every man you meet,
and I am every woman you meet.

Most of us would like to deserve the reputation of being someone who will listen. Not many of us, however, would truly qualify. Nearly everyone can remember at least one instance when someone confided (or bragged), "I'm really a good listener."—And the other person was hard-pressed to stifle the amusement this comment generated; the "good listener" hadn't heard a word spoken to him or her during the entire conversation!

Americans talk "at" each other, not to each other. Sometimes it seems that the objective of talking—communicating—is lost in the attempt to impress ourselves on another.

It would be good for the ego if others considered us good listeners, but that isn't the principal reason for improving ability to listen, to hear. The best reason is a selfish reason. Those who are able to listen well have a dynamic advantage over others who do not.

Studies have proven that nearly 100% of our ability to learn (anything) operates through two senses: Visual and aural. We learn 98% of our life's information by seeing and hearing. This accounts for the awesome effectiveness of TV as a medium for good or evil; TV combines both senses in a tightly-focused "beam" directed at our consciousness... and subconsciousness.

Of the 98% we learn by seeing and hearing, fully 70% of each day's activity is taken up by some form of *communications.* There is no communication without interpersonal relationship of some kind. All day, every day of your life, seven out of every ten minutes will be spent attempting to give or receive information.

How effective you are at both receiving and transmitting information will play a *major role* in how successfully you relate to the world around you. Your *feelings* respond to what you perceive inaccurately; your *thinking mind* responds to what you accurately perceive. We have an English-language expression: "What I *thought* you said was..." —How totally inept that phrase is! It should be, "What I *felt* you said was..."

Of the 70% of our time spent attempting to communicate, it's interestng that we are trained to do best that which we spend least time at; and have virtually no training to do that which takes up *most* of our time.

We spend an average of 9% of our communication time writing.

We devote an average of 16% of our communications time to reading.

Speaking takes up a large share of our communications effort: 30%, on an average.

A whopping 45% of *all* communications effort on the average is devoted to listening...the one element of communications which most of us handle in a slipshod manner.

As you came up through our educational system, you were drilled at writing as if it might be the most important thing you could learn. As it turns out, you use this skill less than 10% of your communications time.

Schools taught you to read, also—although that statement is debatable as to education efficiency in the past 20 to 25 years. At least, they *tried* to get you to read as well as possible, giving it their best shot for eight to ten years. How well you mastered this skill—reading—governs how well you do at some 16% of your communciations.

You *may* have had some speech training—school play, or some such—giving you an edge, a head start on ability to use this 30% of your communication effort more effectively.

Did anyone every try to teach you how to *listen?*

In the past ten or fifteen years, university after university has conducted studies to determine how well entry-level college students listen. The tests invariably show that without some listening training, freshmen students score only 50% recall immediately after hearding a ten-minute talk, and lose 25% of that recall within 48 hours.

It's apparently universal: We manage to "hang onto" about 25% of what we hear after two days have passed. We only use half of what we hear *while we're hearing it!*

We all make an effort to be interesting talkers. We all should be trying to be interesting (interested) listeners! It's a stark fact of life that we want to make good impressions. To make an impression means to be accepted; sometimes it means the difference between profit and loss. It produces a warm glow of self approval when we feel we've done a good job "talking" to someone; and it really bends our ego when we realize that we've done poorly as a conversationalist.

Only an extremely rare individual cares how well we talk. *That's a fact!* A truly great mind, free of self-doubts and the need to feed upon another's ego, is free to pay careful attention to you. You "impress" such a person by what you communicate to him or her. Most of us, however, are not in the "great mind" league. We are more impressed by those who allow us to express ourselves. In other words:

To make an impression on the rarely-encountered mental and emotional "giant:" Talk to him or her, and do it well.

To make an impression on *most people: Listen* to him or her, and *do it well.*

Learning to listen is not something reserved to a fortunate few who "have the talent for it." Listening has almost nothing to do with talent. It is not an attribute we are born with, it is a skill which anyone can master.

First of all: You have to *want to learn.* This means before anything else, you must make an honest and fearless appraisal of your capability. Most people *think* they are good listeners. Studies—literally hundreds of carefully-done research investigations—tell us that very few people listen well. There is probably no way you will increase your listening talent as long as your self-image leads you to believe you already are a good listener.

The steps to learning to listen are relatively few and very simple. Perhaps they're too simple: We tend to overlook the obvious and give little effort toward the simple. Essentially, if each of us diligently studied the following list of listening "disabilities" and worked at changing our own approach to minimize them, we'd all be much better listeners.

Inattention. Paying attention is difficult at times. We have all mastered numerous "body English" signals we use to tell another person we are paying attention—when precisely the opposite is true. The relaxed pose, chin rested in cupped hand, the level gaze, the nodding head: All of these are meant to say, "keep talking; I'm listening."

Listening is *not* a relaxed, effortless activity. The word "attention" should be split into two parts: "at tension," to signify the intent, focused, highly-channeled energy that accompanies good listening. In order to listen well enough to really hear what the other person is saying (and sometimes, what he or she is NOT saying), means we have to give up one of the activities we usually are engaged in while pretending to listen:

Rehearsing. Planning what we're going to say next, when it's again "our turn to talk," is one of the principal culprits leading to inattention. You *know* someone is listening to you when you conclude a thought and ask, "How do you feel about what I've just said?" and the other person responds:

"I dunno. Let me think about it for a moment."

Typically, you wouldn't *have* to ask. Most conversations are like tennis matches: One person bats a thought across the net and the other slams it right back. If someone was listening to you so carefully he or she hadn't formed *any* response, you may be sure the person was listening to you "at tension." One of the things that leads to *rehearsing* instead of listening is:

Becoming Emotionally Involved. How we we need to watch for this disability! Communications experts use the term "buzz words" for those unfortunate expressions that ignite our emotions and turn off our listeners. For example: Suppose that a woman is listening to an expert on some aspect of interior design. It's important that she pay close attention, because the expert can impart information which will make a difference in the woman's income as a home decorator. The woman (who is chapter president of the local National Organization for Women) is doing very well until the speaker uses the term, "dumb broads."

Buzz! Veins begin to throb the temple, the eyes narrow, and the emotions become a seething cauldron.

The woman begins to plan when and how she will cut this person down to size. No matter how much she paid to hear this particular expert in her own field, she might as well ask for a refund for everything following the buzz words "dumb broads." She didn't hear the rest of it!

The speaker's opinion of sexual inequality had nothing to do with his ability as a design expert, and it had no bearing on the woman's capacity to learn or to perform. She'd have been far, far ahead of the game if she'd mentally hurled a comback ("stupid jerk!") and went right on listening to the message.

Any time we hear something that triggers an emotional reaction we need to *very quickly* ascertain:

1. Did the speaker intentionally use the buzz word to antagonize? If the other person isn't "trying to pick a fight," there's nothing to gain if we begin emotionally fighting with him or her.

2. Am I being subjected to a personal attack? —Did the speaker mean what he or she said in the same light as my immediate interpretation of it?

3. Did the buzz word set me off on a tangent? Am I now beginning to think and rehearse my reply along lines which have nothing to do with the actual topic?

IF necessary for your own emotional/rational well-being, when you realize you are reacting emotionally to something the other person said, do one of two things:

Interrupt; explain what's bothering you, and let the other person respond, or: Shut up and listen, forcing your feelings to back away from whatever the other person said that...well...hurt your feelings.

Creating or permitting distractions is a listening disability which can be overcome. The obvious distractions are those we create: Working with the hands while (supposedly) listening; dividing our attention between the speaker and a TV set or radio, "hiding" behind a newspaper. How many times has someone pleaded with you to "Put that damn thing down and *listen* to me!"?

The distractions we permit are more subtle, but no

less of an impairment to complete listening. Typical of these is our preoccupation with the speaker's physical appearance, or mannerisms. If someone is trying to communicate in a singsong voice, or so emotionally he or she does poorly in marshalling ideas and presenting them, we are prone to become critical of the speaker. This puts us on a tangent: Part of the mind is busy analyzing the other person's appearance or delivery and criticizing him or her for it.

When we permit any disconcerting influence to come between our purpose (listening) and our attention, our efficiency plummets. Because most of us are unskilled and inexperienced at listening well, we cannot afford this efficiency loss if we are to comprehend, particularly if it is important that we hear both what the other person is saying and what he or she is *not* saying.

Learn to identify your personality type with your listening habits: It will pay huge dividends. Because each of us is most comfortable when listening to another of the same personality characteristics, it follows that we begin to lose efficiency rapidly when we are trying to listen to someone whose style is *not* in our personal "comfort zone."

A *pusher* has an extraordinary sense of time passing and is personally oriented toward facts and conclusions. He or she will be uncomfortable listening to an *examiner's* conversation. The examiner will want to paint in all of the background and enumerate all of the alternatives. Time invested in developing "the big picture" is, to an examiner, time well spent. To a pusher, it is time painfully wasted.

The extroverted, assertive *outspoken* may be the poorest-suited personality style for listening. This person will leap ahead of the speaker, interrupt, change the subject; never realizing that he or she is depriving the other person of an opportunity to express himself. The *outspoken* and the *examiner* both share one listening problem: Either of these personality types is frequently guilty of planning what he or she will say next, instead of listening while the other person is taking a turn.

The *outspoken* is probably most susceptible to becoming thrown off the track by "buzz words." These emotionally volatile folks frequently pick one word out of context and jump on it, like a dog on a bone. The flow of conversation comes to an abrupt halt while we go off "into the weeds" to discuss the offending buzz word.

"—Wait a minute!" the *outspoken* interrupts, "Just what did you mean by that crack you just made?"

"—What crack?" asks the genuinely bewildered speaker. There had been no hidden meaning, no personal application of the word: It simply triggered the outspoken, who *immediately* lost the train of thought.

In earlier chapters we made the point that there is no one better personality style; and that whatever your personal style is, it is best for you.

We described what happens when each personality type is driven out of his or her "comfort zone" into emotional stages of reaction and over-reaction. How, then, do we cope with this when we are listening to someone who "drives us up a wall?"

The key is that we can function very well for specified periods outside of our comfort zone *if we are aware we are doing it.* When we don't realize what's happening, the automatic progression from discomfort to reaction sets in and seriously interrupts our listening ability. If we learn (and we can) to watch for the internal signals of personal discomfort, it becomes relatively easy to "match" the speaker's style for as long as necessary to get the conversation concluded.

This by no means implies that an outspoken can become a sensitive; a pusher can become a examiner, or that any one of us can "become" something we are not. We *can* control our own reaction to another person, however. Watch for the sensation that you "don't like" the way another person talks: It's a dead give-away that he or she is of a different personality style than you.

When you discover this sensation, which begins as a mild irritation and becomes distractingly uncomfortable, it is the key to "lock in" on what the other is saying and *listen*. If you don't redouble your efforts to listen carefully, the growing discomfort will edge you toward personality "backfire."

Becoming bored. This listening problem is virtually universal. Why is it that we are *never* bored with what we have to say, but are frequently bored by what we have to listen to? Is it possible that each of us is more intelligent than the rest of us? —Hardly likely. One of the contributing factors here is the time-differential between speech speed and thinking speed.

We talk, at an average, about 125 words per minute. We can think, ordinarily, at some 400 words per minute. Unless the speaker and the subject really tax our brainpower, we are usually running off ahead of the speaker. By the time he or she completes half a sentence, we are ready to interrupt with words or body English telling him or her we understand.

It's easy to "check in" with the speaker about every fourth or fifth word, to make sure we're still "with him," and then mentally wander off to think about something else. Whether that "something else" is our next conversational gambit or the high price of cauliflower makes little difference: The speaker usually can read our body English, which signals that we're bored. This can be disasterous to communications.

Depending on personality, when we become bored we either interrupt or shut down the conversation; or we fidget and squirm, or become immobile and expressionless. A bored sensitive really has a problem: He or she doesn't want to listen, but neither does a sensitive want to hurt the other person's feelings. Usually, the sensitive takes on a burlesque of a listening attitude when bored: They'll become so involved with "looking like they're listening" the the speaker is disconcerted.

We become bored easily when the subject matter is difficult and the speaker not particularly expressive. Albert Einstein was not a dynamic speaker. It's highly likely that he would have bored the authors in a discussion of his theories. Just because Dr. Nara and Steve Mariner can't handle a concept as tough as $E=MC^2$ hardly makes the subject boring.

Remember: *There are no boring speakers; just bored listeners.* When you catch yourself becoming bored while listening, you have only two options:

1. Decide you and the speaker will get nothing of value from the communication and end it, or
2. Decide it's important that you *or* the speaker find something of value in the communication, and *pay attention.*

Being fact-happy. All of us suffer this listening disease to some extent. We listen for facts, collecting them the way squirrels collect nuts. This listening habit, perhaps a hold-over from school days, is one of the principal enemies of real understanding. People *talk* in facts, true: Facts are the word-bricks used to build *concepts*. It is virtually impossible to speak in completed concepts and much of our communication is used to paint "word pictures." Separate words and phrases, thoughts and sentences, are like the brush strokes used to paint the picture which, when done, will be an entire concept.

Our memories are like sieves when we try to store facts as if they were an assortment of nuts and bolts. We learn and comprehend and remember *concepts*, not individual facts.

If someone told another person about a new inventory-control system, would the listener understand the concept or would he be "derailed" by a fact—"we frequently run out of widgets on the assembly line," for example. If the hearer was listening for facts, he or she would still be trying to decide what to do about the widget problem when the speaker concluded with, "What do you think of my idea?"

"—What idea? ...Listen, if we've having a widget problem, maybe we ought to be thinking about an inventory-control system. What do you think?"

"...huh?"

For more than one-third of the rest of your life you will be involved in the specific communications function called, for want of a better term, "listening." It is the *one* communication skill for which you are least prepared by training and experience. It is *not* a talent.

People who appear to be "talented" at listening are those who learned how accidentally, or through training in a related field such as counseling. The greater majority of us are lousy listeners; but not because "that's the way we are." Listening is a skill anyone can develop.

Your listening equipment is already installed, ready to operate "at the flip of a switch." You needn't go to a special school, or try to learn a dogma or rules for better listening. All you need is a sincere desire—and a great deal of effort, because becoming a good listener takes practice, experience, and hard work.

In real life, the good talkers are the unskilled labor; the good listeners are the communications professionals. Think about what you want to get out of life, and then think about the "pay scale" difference between unskilled labor and professionalism. Remembering that more than one third of your life will involve you in this business of "listening," what return do you expect for your "investment" of time?

Finally: If you need any further incentive to become a better listener, consider the result of a large-scale industrial study made a few years ago: The researchers set out to discover what one single management skill was most important for human relations. By a tremendous margin, the "winner" was expressed in some variation of this statement:

"I like my boss. I can talk to him (her)."

No single human activity involves as much of our time as listening. It is the one communication skill we are least prepared for.

Sounds like a good application for the 180-Degree Theory, doesn't it?

Chapter Eleven

"*Problems, Pathwatchers & A Razor*"

(*Some Thoughts About Thinking*)

Everybody knows how to think, unless he or she is beyond senile or genuinely stupid. Since neither of those types is likely to read *The 180-Degree Theory,* we can assume the reader can think. However, the theme of this book is that most of us have grown accustomed to "thinking" with our intestines as well as our brains: We employ emotional processes mixed with rational processes and call that mixture, loosely, "thinking."

Wrong!

Thinking requires zero input from our feelings. In fact, when *any* contamination of feelings is present, the result is something less than pure thought...and that's where we run into problems. Problems, fortunately, can be overcome.

First, however: It is necessary to learn to distinguish between a *problem* and a *circumstance or condition.* If you were walking along a sidewalk and a big flowerpot fell fourteen stories directly onto your head, you would *not* have a problem. You most certainly would have a condition; and would be the victim of a circumstance. The circumstance is real: Something fell and hit you on the head. The condition is equally real: You just got killed. Problem? —Not at all. *There is no solution for that circumstance, and no possible change of that condition.*

A *problem* is a situation which confronts us; a situation which can be overcome by identifying the solution. Problems can't exist without solutions. Perhaps the solutions are difficult to find, but there will be some way—or even alternative ways—of resolving an issue when it is truly a problem.

We make a grave mistake and expend a lot of useless effort trying to find the solutions to life's *circumstances.* Circumstances don't necessarily have solutions. The way things *are* can be an insurmountable reality. When a circumstance or set of circumstances has no solution, it is *not* a problem. You could go nuts trying to solve such a puzzle.

When we're faced with a set of circumstances which are bad for us, we become more and more emotional as we grapple for an answer to "the problem" —rational thought divorced from emotion would save emotional wear and tear. We should develop the knack of asking ourselves, "Is this a problem or a circumstance?" If it is a problem, we can usually think of the solution. If it's a circumstance, there may be nothing we can do about it except worry...and, of course, worry is just another name for anxiousness. That will breed anxiety, something none of us need to manufacture purposely.

A retailer friend of Dr. Bob's once got into a cash-flow "crunch" just before his peak selling season. If he went into the season without a large stock inventory, he would lose many thousands of dollars in sales. Because his business had grown—too quickly—for three years, his line of credit with banks and commercial houses was inadequate to cover the inventory he needed.

The circumstance: He needed $50,000 additional credit and nobody would advance it for him.

The man was emotionally determined to "think it out" for himself. After several days, Dr. Bob asked him what the trouble was. He replied, "Oh, I've got a problem...but I'll work it out. I just need time."

The following day he passed out and was taken to the hospital. He was on the thin edge of a mental and physical breakdown. Trying to solve his "problem" had come very near destroying *any* hope for business that year.

When Dr. Bob visited him in the hospital, the man finally explained his situation. He concluded his story with the words, "So that's my problem, Bob; and I don't know what to do about it."

"No," Dr. Bob replied, "That *isn't* a problem. That's a circumstance, Charlie, and there is nothing you *can* do about it. If it was a problem, you could settle it somehow. As a circumstance, the only thing that can help you is a change in the circumstances...and the change has to come from someone else."

Then and there, a limited partnership arrangement was worked out. Dr. Bob agreed to act as co-guarantor for the expanded line of credit the merchant needed, to tide him through the coming season.

When he talks about this as an illustration of the difference between a problem and a circumstance, Dr. Bob points out that if the man had understood the difference *before* he almost destroyed his health worrying, he would have told Dr. Bob earlier what his trouble was.

"Had Charlie known he *couldn't* solve the 'problem,' he would have asked for help. Emotionally, he was determined to find the answer by himself; he couldn't abide the thought of being beaten by a problem. It wasn't a problem. The difference is more than important: It's vital."

And that brings us to that curious word in this chapter title, "razor." In the first half of the thirteenth century, in England, there was a philosopher named William of Occam. He was credited for stating a principal of logic (thought) which says that in explaining anything, *the fewest possible assumptions* are to be used. The principal is called "Occam's Razor," and you can use it to shave a lot of excess worry from your life.

Assumptions are necessary, because we seldom have the luxury of knowing all the facts in any situation. We are required frequently to make a decision based on a mixture of known facts...and assumptions. Occam's

Razor is used to shave as many assumptions from the process as possible.

In any given situation, the facts will point to various conclusions which can be reached. Assumptions will "fill in the blanks" between facts. Once we've completed the mental inventory of facts and assumptions, we've reached the critical point in the decision process.

This is the point where feelings enter the picture. We now view the overall situation with a built-in tendency to see things the way we want them to be, instead of the way they factually happen to be.

Another way of stating Occam's principle is that when you have examined the alternatives, the one which most closely fits all known facts is probably the correct one.

In any life situation, Occam's Razor is good to remember when you're analyzing the background. Your feelings will prompt you to make assumptions. Feelings cannot alter facts, however; so paying more attention to fact than assumption is a function of the thinking mind.

Don't try to "solve" circumstances; don't assume you can't solve a problem. Every time you catch yourself thinking that you're not doing too badly under the circumstances, immediately ask yourself, "What am I doing under these circumstances?" In your life—in my life—in everyone's life, sooner or later we become enmeshed in circumstances we can't change. Often, the only "solution" is to get out from under that set of circumstances.

Another serious barrier to thinking, and particularly to implementing the thoughts, is our constant concern over what other people will think.

That's right: Even those among us who reacted to that last sentence by murmuring, "Not me, baby...I don't care what other people think!" —even those folks are affected by this emotional quirk.

We are all conformists to varying degrees. To be a total nonconformist would subject us to social ostracism. What others think of us determines their reaction to our presence in society. We *must* be concerned with what others think of us, because we put points on life's scoreboard only when others consider our value or lack of it. What we deserve is established by what others think of us. Like it or not, "what others think" is of significant effect on our own pursuit of happiness.

However: "Others" spend precious little time "thinking" of us at all; good or bad. Everyone is preoccupied with his or her own problems and desires. To break through that preoccupation with self and get people to consider us, instead, is not easy. We must do something very good—or very bad—to "get attention." As a general rule, each of us places far too much emphasis on what we *feel* others may *think* of us. We allow this consideration to color all of our thoughts and actions when in fact, it ought to influence only a very small portion of our thinking.

There's a second curious word in this chapter title: Pathwatchers. What are "pathwatchers," anyway?

Years ago a man told us about his pathwatcher theory. He said that life is like a path which people follow, well-traveled and smooth. We can negotiate the path easily because hundreds of thousands of people have preceded us, wearing it smooth. Not only is the going easy, but there is someone just ahead of us to be followed; and somone ahead of that person, and someone ahead of...

As long as you keep your head down and just follow blindly, nobody will notice you. "They" won't "think" about you if you blend in with everyone else.

Well off to the sides of the path, however, there are other follks: They are pathwatchers. They come and go as they please, keeping an eye on the multitude walking the pathway. If someone steps a little ways off the path; gets out of line in any way, the pathwatcher will step forward and motion for the straying individual to get back in line.

"All you have to do," our friend said, "Is take a giant step off the path. If you take small steps; if you're hesitant, the pathwatchers will order you back in line. But if you take a quantum leap, you're suddenly among the pathwatchers. They don't ask whether you belong there. You're there, so you *must be* another pathwatcher."

He told us he developed this image once—the concept of the ordinary pathwalkers and the extraordinary pathwatchers—and puzzled over how you could become a pathwatcher.

"The realization hit me like a burst of light," he said. "There's no selection system for pathwatchers. Nobody earns the right. They just step off the path and become pathwatchers...anyone can do it."

Others will notice you, in life, whenever you do anything exceptional. The one thing we cannot be forgiven is to succeed where others fail. Short of outrageous, nonsensical behavior the quickest way to get attention is to appear different in a *sensible* way.

To achieve mental self-sufficiency will turn you into a pathwatcher: You will no longer be required to follow everyone else down life's path. You can come and go within reason as you please, answerable only to your own best judgment whether your actions are good for you and others.

It is a waste of time to brood over whether others will "like you." Some people will; some won't. Remember: They, too, are mixtures of feelings and thinking. The human animal is not a fully-rational entity. Whether others will like you or dislike you is partly a function of what you do with your life; and partly a function of how they perceive it.

In the proliferation of self-help books lining our bookstore shelves, we are inundated with those books wanting to teach us about "self." They seem to be split just about in three types:

One school of thought wants you to become self-realized so that everyone will like you.

Another wants you to take charge of your self and to hell with whether others like you or not.

The third group wants to teach you how you, yourself, can control everyone else so they have to like you.

In this preoccupation with "self," isn't it interesting how all of these systems rely so heavily on the reactions of others as a gauge of "self" improvement?

"Be selfish," these methods seem to tell us, "And check with other people to see how well you're doing."

180 degrees away from that: Be socially responsible, be compassionate and considerate of your fellows, and *think for yourself* to see how well you're doing.

Self-improvement, if it is successful at all, ultimately benefits those around us. It requires a certain concentration on self in order to effect improvements; but the more we mature, we place less and less value on "self," and more value on others. Earlier in our emotional development we tend to place a premium on what others think, and tailor our actions accordingly. As we progress, we are less and less concerned with what others think, but tailor our actions for the greater good.

Alan Briskin of University of Minnesota discussed the implications of this in an article in *The Cooperative Builder,* December, 1974. Psychologist Briskin said there appear to be six levels of "ethical-moral development," levels of ability to respond to the world around us in a mature, thoughtful manner.

Stage one is the first level with any ethics or morals. A newborn infant has *zero* moral relationship with the world around it: It is toally self-centered. In stage one a person is concerned with punishment; "conscience" consists of behaving in ways to keep from being punished. People in this stage obey the law solely out of fear of being caught and fined or jailed if they don't. There is no sense of right or wrong; only the evaluation of "safe" and "punishable" conduct.

In stage two people react out of desire for reward or benefit. A threat to their property values would be considered more important than giving others an opportunity to live in freedom. People acting at this stage, Briskin said, probably wouldn't experience any guilt from actions that might hurt others, as long as they themselves profit from those actions.

Proving that ethical/moral development has no real tie to age or intelligence, Briskin pointed out that Adolph Hitler—a genius; a fully-grown adult—could not possibly have evolved beyond stage one or two.

"Good boy, good girl" is Briskin's definition of stage three. Such people are conformists who actively seek approval from their society. What the neighbors think becomes the prime consideration and stage three people are deeply involved with their "image" and keeping up appearances.

Stage four development is called "The law and order stage" by psychological researchers. People at this level have a high regard for social law and will be more concerned with rules than with "what others think."

Stage three people look up to stage four people. According to Briskin:

> In the last presidential election people were offered law and order by Nixon and Agnew. In order to be 'good boys and girls' many of them voted for this offer. Conformists often do not like to think for themselves. Law and order morality allows people to defer to authority without having to think about it.

The *Cooperative Builder* article concluded with a thought so chilling, and so appropriate to our theme of becoming mentally self-sufficient, we'll quote it verbatim:

> Two higher stages have been found to exist above the law and order stage. As a given individual progresses to these stages, a heightened "sense of

self'' is developed.

This greater awareness requires the person to think about his or her own actions. Deference to any authority as a reason for action falls away and the basic ''rightness'' of an action is considered. At stage five, a long-run point of view involving self-respect and the greater good of the community is developed.

At stage six, the person becomes governed by very broad moral principles. Here, a law may be deliberately violated in order to achieve justice, as in the actions of such men as Martin Luther King and Mahatma Ghandi. Both men, for example, believed that ''The only true liberation is that which frees both oppressor and oppressed.''

Researchers are troubled over the finding that possibly over half of the U.S. adult population is at or below the conformity level, or stage three. If this is so, at least half of the U.S. population could be expected to defer to authority without thinking through the implications of such actions.

As you consider this, evaluate to what extent in your own life ''what other people think'' colors your feelings and influences your thinking. As you become more and more adept at the 180-Degree Theory, you should experience a shifting in your viewpoint:

You will be concerned less and less about what others think; and you will think more and more *about* others. It will be less important for them to like you and more important for you to ''like'' them.

This concept of ethical/moral development sheds light on the ''pathwatcher theory.'' If it's true that more than half of us are at or below ethical/moral stage three, then the bulk of the people moving up and down the path are well-suited to being *followers.* Conformists and people who are constantly aware of "the rules" would spend very little time thinking a situation through to its ethical or moral conclusion.

While the "pathwatcher" illustration is highly imaginative—there aren't *really* people standing off to one side herding most of us up and down a path—wouldn't it be comforting to hope that, were it true, most of the pathwatchers were developed to stage five or six?

You can't be both an innovator and a conformist at the same time. You will find it very difficult to *think* about your actions so long as your thinking is clouded by feelings about your "image" with other people.

Thinking —the art and science of using your head and not your feelings —involves many things. You will have a clear "head start" (no pun intended) on thinking, however, if you apply these broad principles:

Don't confuse "problems" with "circumstances." If you set out to solve a problem, make sure you are convinced there *is* a solution.

Sharpen up "Occam's Razor" and use it constantly: Thinking, making decisions, *demands* that you work with facts as much as possible; with as few assumptions as possible, and with virtually *no* emotions.

Become a "pathwatcher." Your thinking will influence your actions, and your actions will have an effect on other people's lives. Become guided by moral and ethical principles; spend less time with concern for what others will think. Note that there is less and less room for pure thinking at the lower ends of the moral/ethical scale; more and more *need* for thinking at the upper end.

If you are guided by fear of punishment, driven by the need for acceptance, guided by desire for rewards...all you need to do is "follow the path." You don't *have* to stay on it, though.

Psychologist Briskin's comments about ethical/moral development included this encouragement:

> No one need be stuck at a low level of ethical intelligence for life. Solving life's dilemmas, experienceing conflict, desiring to improve, becoming concerned for others, all these things can stimulate the development of ethical intelligence to higher levels.

In other words, becoming mentally *self*-sufficient is the most *un*-selfish goal you can achieve in life. By now it should come as no surprise that the truth is 180 degrees from where at first it seemed to be...

Let's pretend you are a lower-level executive employed by the Didier Company of Berlin. You've risen quite rapidly within the firm; there's talk over the water cooler that you are favored for a mangement position.

Not that you don't deserve it! You've been loyal, you've worked hard. You have always taken as much of your own off-duty time as necessary to study and understand the products Didier Company manufactures. You get along well with others, both those senior to you and the growing number of people who report to you.

With the 1941 economy booming, Didier Company is doing very well...and your personal star is rising right along with the company's fortunes.

You've made it a point to avoid politics as much as you can, knowing that two of the most dangerous topics are politics and religion. It would have been a blunder to offend people in authority by making an offhand remark that could come home to roost at the next personnel evaluation.

Attention to work, careful handling of yourself in dealing with the executives and remaining fair and open with those under you has paid off. Last Monday you were promoted to fill a vacancy as manager of the industrial relations and sales office. True, the promotion was specifically described as "temporary," and your title is "acting department chief" —but it's not beyond reason to hope that it will become permanent.

This Monday you handled your first really big problem. Naturally, the government is one of Didier's biggest customers: A single sale and installation can amount to a full year's purchases from private buyers.

You worked out all of the details, projected the costs. You discussed it with the production people, with engineering; even got a virtual "go-ahead" from one of the company vice-presidents. Then, you dictated the letter which will go to the government's purchasers. If it works, it will virtually guarantee your permanent promotion.

All you have to do is sign the letter when the secretary finishes typing it. It will go out in this afternoon's mail. You wish there wasn't a queasy feeling in the pit of your stomach. Oh, there's nothing to worry about as far as the order is concerned: You did your homework well enough for that—you'll make the sale.

It's just that...well, dammit! —All those people...

That's enough of that! There *is* a war on, and if Didier wasn't involved another company would be. And if *you* don't complete this assignment, someone else *will.*

The secretary brings the letter into your office and centers it on your desk. You lean forward, not touching it, and read it slowly, carefully:

> Gentlemen:
>
> We acknowledge the receipt of your order for five triple furnaces including two electric elevators for raising the corpses.
>
> We suggest using a simple metal forklift for transporting the bodies into the furnaces; we do not believe conveyor apparatus is indicated.
>
> Revised plans for the new installa-

tion of cremation ovens, coal-fired, are attached.

We are able to unconditionally guarantee their effectiveness and durability as well as our use of finest materials and our faultless workmanship.

The Didier Company
Berlin (1941)

For a moment (only a moment) the stark meaning of the words you dictated makes you pause. Then, resolutely, you reach for the pen and sign the letter.

At the door, on her way out, the secretary turns and asks, "What did you say, Sir?"

"Nothing, nothing" you reply, waving her away. You had not realized that you'd spoken aloud: A combination prayer, excuse, and reminder that a man looks out for Number One:

"...I only work here—"

The letter you just read is an exact transcription of one sent by Didier Company of Berlin, in 1941. The story woven around the letter is a chracterization, but it could very well be true in all but only highly significant respect.

The only complete fiction in that story is that *you* dictated that letter. We can be grateful that you were not actually there...

...Or were you? Weren't we *all* —humanity itself—in that Berlin office in 1941?

We've been considering something called "ethical and emotional maturity" in this chapter. Please think about this some more, in light of your brief "assignment" with the Didier Company. Think about how we transported you to a different time and place, just long enough to have to make a choice between your career and your conscience.

This time, we gave you a chance to practice; but life in the raw hands us such choices with no practice runs. Life is played "live," not taped for later broadcast.

Pressures of society can be enormous; often with only our intuition (conscience) in opposition. Making social choices demands *thinking*, not emotions. An emotionally-mature intuition, coupled with reason, simply could not accept the excuse, "If I don't, someone else will...besides, I only work here."

Chapter Twelve

"What Are We NOW Gonna Do?"

Those of Finnish extraction (Dr. Bob Nara, for example), or those familiar with Finnish-American speech patterns, might have gotten a chuckle from this chapter title. The intentional mis-placement of the word "now" gives this question an added dimension; a sense of immediate urgency simply not present in the question, "What are we going to do now?"

With typical Finnish economy, these folks have taken an ordinary expression and made it over into one which emphasizes two points:

—What are we going to do, and

—Starting with this moment; immediately: Now.

What are we NOW going to do about the 180-Degree Theory? We've been together through many chapters explaining some psychology, some interpersonal relationshps, some things such as learning to listen. We've talked about the mind as having, for our purposes, three separate "divisions," the thinking mind, the feelings factory, and the plant maintenance division.

If we've done absolutely nothing else other than to convince you that you suffer when you attempt to think and make decisions with your emotions, the book has been beneficial.

We'd like the book to help you with much more than this. Each of the preceding chapters contained a concept that can stand by itself; something you can use in your personal quest for mental self-sufficiency. In most cases, the independent concepts you've just read about become even more powerful when modified and influenced by the others.

The chapter about personality types, for instance, can answer many self-questions about why you act—and react—as you do; and why others are different. The chapter describing the function of the subconscious—the feelings factory—explains in general how *everyone's* cognitive/conative think-tank operates. When you add these two chapters together, personalized for yourself, the total is more than simple addition. The effect of pooling all of this information is *synergistic:* "The joint action of agents...that when, taken together, increase each other's effectiveness."

You've already learned more than you may be aware of. As you read your subconscious stores information while your conscious mind "chews on it." The process of teaching the cognitive mind to dominate the conative has already begun, even without specific effort on your part.

Why? —As this information was being processed the subconscious was exposed to an outline of how it is *supposed to* function. As we've pointed out, the subconscious cannot make distinctions as to the validity of a concept. It will believe anything we feed into it. So the part of the 180-Degree Theory which places the thinking mind back in control has already been assimilated by the subconscious and stored in the "memory banks."

All we need to do now is find the "activate" switch, put a fingertip, so to speak, on that button, and push.

That's what we're now gonna do.

We've taken pains to describe the 180-Degree Theory as a vehicle used to achieve mental self-sufficiency: It is no overnight panacea for all personality problems. You won't be remarkably different tomorrow from what you are today; you'll be changed in *very small* ways, completely invisible to those you know and associate with. You probably won't notice any difference in yourself, either. You'll know the 180-Degree Theory is working, however. Daily you will see evidence, in the lives and actions of those around you, of how *not* using these principles lessens mental self-sufficiency.

Every time you notice such an example—so commonplace you simply "didn't see them" before—you'll be reinforcing your own conscious *and subconscious* awareness of what you are trying to do in your own life.

You should begin immediately using some of these concepts in practical and selfish ways. Learning how to master your own personality-reaction to avoid listening emotionally (poorly) to someone who yesterday would "drive you up a wall" will pay huge dividends. Go ahead: Be selfish; learn to listen for your own benefit. How on earth can this kind of selfishness be criticized? The world desperately needs more capable listeners. Becoming adept at hearing what people say—and don't say—will benefit you and others around you, too.

Way early in this book we suggested that you avoid any interpersonal relationship—any game—which required that someone "lose." The beauty of being a selfish listener is that *everybody wins.*

Before a navigator makes any attempt to chart a course to a chosen destination he or she first determines exactly where presently located. To go somewhere specific, instead of simply wandering and trusting luck to arrive safely, we need a starting point; we need to know where we are now, how fast we can travel, where we are trying to go and how distant that point is.

In other words, we need to orient ourselves.

How secure are you, today? Mental self-sufficiency, a sense of wellbeing, is based on a secure foundation. It is no accident that the Salvation Army and Communist guerrillas employ a similar technique: Both of these provide people with food, clothing and shelter before attempting to persuade them regarding spiritual or social concepts. Ideas are wasted on empty stomachs.

We don't imply that the 180-Degree Theory is limited to those whose physical life is in order. On the contrary, these principles can be put to use by anyone, anywhere, under any circumstances. Remember Mr. Liebman's brief essay on wellbeing? He mentioned that

> "...yet, on the other hand, I have seen this inner tranquility flourish without the material supports of property or even the blessings of physical health. Peace of Mind is not something that can be bought..."

Nevertheless, it is seldom disputed among psychologists that people seem to act/react in life based on a scale of human needs. We progress upward in social-mental-emotional levels only as the more basic needs are filled.

Security is the first, most basic human need. Food, shelter and clothing—or the acquisition of these—would occupy all of our efforts until these three needs were met.

In America our lifestyle has replaced these "basic" needs with another set of "basic" needs, no less necessary. Now we more or less accept these primitive needs as our birthright: We've moved on and upwards. Now we seek more exotic food in quantities we don't really need; we want not simply shelter, but a "nice home" and clothing has become a sort of badge we wear to show others our identity...our status in society, or our militant unconcern for society, as in ragged bluejeans and shaggy hair.

These are *physical* needs. Once we've become relatively secure that these needs are cared for, or will be, we then address social needs.

Normal people, as soon as the stomach is full and they are shielded from the rain, next begin to feel an "itch" that is scratched only by some very personal interpersonal relationships with a member of the opposite sex.

Call that step one, then: The cave-man dragging a not-really-struggling woman toward a cave, where there's a cheerful fire burning and fresh game roasting. Having fulfilled all of his needs, you'd think the cave-man would be satisfied.

180 degrees away from that first thought: Picture this fellow a few hours later, seated at the entrance to his cave. He's warm and well-fed and there is a soft, cuddly "she" within easy reach. If he had a developed language, he could put into words the feelings that have captured his attention:

"I wonder..."

...and a *concept* is born.

We have all progressed beyond step one. Now we spend most of our waking hours prodded by some variation of "I wonder..." —a constant, restless appraisal and re-appraisal of who we are, why we're here, and what we want from life.

We've achieved an acceptable—perhaps temporary—level of physical security. For most of us there is a gnawing dis-satisfaction with our physical achievements: We are a nation of hungry people. We want more money, bigger houses, newer cars, fatter bank accounts. Even those of us who have no desire to become wealthy would certainly like to achieve a socio-financial level we'd describe as "enough."

Many of us have long-ago reached the conclusion that "if I had these things, I'd have peace of mind." Wrong! At no point in the entire 180-Degree Theory is there a much more important principle. *Things* do not bring about mental self-sufficiency. The reverse (as usual) is true: Those who find mental maturity, or peace of mind, usually discover that the "things" in life either lose importance, or are more easily acquired...or both.

In 1923 a group of the world's most successful financial giants met at a hotel in Chicago. Among those present:

—President of the largest utility company—Samuel Insull

—President of the largest gas company—Howard Hopson

—The leading wheat speculator-Arthur Cutton

—President, New York Stock Exchange—Richard Whitney

—Member of the Presidential Cabinet—Albert Fall

Wall Street "Bear"—Jesse Livermore

—Boss of the world's leading monopoly—Iven Kruger

—President, International Settlement Bank—Charles Schwab

By 1948—after 25 years had passed—this is a measure of how much mental self-sufficiency these great fortunes had produced:

Samuel Insull died a penniless fugitive in a foreign country; unable to return to the U.S.

Howard Hopson went insane.

Arthur Cutton died abroad, his fortune evaporated.

Richard Whitney tried to piece together his life after release from Sing Sing penitentiary.

Albert Fall was pardoned from prison so he could, mercifully, die in peace at home.

Jesse Livermore committed suicide.

Iven Kruger committed suicide.

Charles Schwab died bankrupt and in debt.

These men, who had learned well the art of making money, apparently had learned little or nothing about human relations and the art of living successfully and happily. Let's count our days and not our dollars; learn to smell the flowers along the way. (From

Dr. Robert Nara's original publication, *Feelings.*)

Having financial security in life is about equally important as the security which derives from sexual fulfillment and the need for a level of control over our life-styles. For better or worse; money, sex and power seem to be the bearings upon which the axle of life turns. So many people have devoted near-obsessive effort to achieve some or all of these, only to discover (as in the list above) that *genuine* success must be founded on peace of mind.

We are concerned, therefore, with the *other* kind of security everyone needs: *Emotional* security. It is incredibly difficult to achieve any measure of success in physical "markers" —money, prestiege, power—if we are not *first* successful within ourselves. Even those who manage to obtain life's *things*, without first becoming mentally self-sufficient, seem unable to enjoy them or retain them.

Perhaps there is some natural or supernatural principle operating about which we know nothing; we perceive only the effects of this principle when viewing the list of "successful failures" on the preceding pages. The list continues, of course: Adolph Hitler was successful until he died an insane syphilitic who had slaughtered 6,000,000 people while trying to achieve physical success for the "master race."

Shakespeare wrote: "To thine own self be true; and it follows as the night follows day that you cannot be false to others."

A psychologist years ago penned an equation: E(W)-D. *Everybody wants dignity,* he said. Dignity is a sense of personal wellbeing, a sure and certain appraisal of our inner self as having met, and passed, the test of life. A person with true dignity does not need to strive for attention. He or she is not "trying to *be* somebody;" he or she *is* somebody.

A down-and-out hobo dressed in rags can magically transform a park bench into a throne; a hot dog into a feast—by lending *dignity* to these simple surroundings. Secure in his belief that the world is spinning essentially the way God planned it; that he is a child of the universe...neither the best or the worst...with a *right* to be here—the lowliest "bum" may have achieved a measure of success for which others would trade a fortune...

That inner glow of mental self-sufficiency comes after we have progressed upward on the "scale of needs" from simple security to the realm of the conceptual.

We begin with basic emotional security—with our "feelings" under control—and progress to our *purpose* in life. Why am I here? What am I meant to leave behind that will prove I once passed this way? Unless I am content to wander aimlessly, drifting on the sea of life, I must have some *purpose*; some goal.

Having considered my purpose in life and decided that I can and should try to achieve it, I then progress to the next level: I become involved with *achievement.* During the period of being an achiever, I will rely on others to help me inventory my progress.

I will then be in the *reward* level of development. For my efforts on behalf of myself and my fellow humans, I have a right to expect some form of reward. (I *deserve* it.)

Recognition follows reward. At this level of emotional development the "points on the scoreboard" become more subtle. Now we are not measuring progress in material things or semi-material things (promotions, salary increases, etc.). The progress becomes marked by *recognition;* the "points" are now *conceptual.* The person is known as "having it together," he or she becomes respected. It makes no difference whether the recognition is international—the person is famous—or contained within the individual's neighborhood.

He or she has achieved dignity. Not only is he or she secure internally; having become self-recognized, this person now also can rely on recognition coming from others through interpersonal relationships.

Having achieved mental and emotional self-sufficiency and arrived at a *conceptual* level, this person is now a candidate for emotional maturity stages five and six, discussed in the preceding chapter:

> This greater awareness requires the person to think about his or her own actions. Deference to any authorty as a reason for action falls away and the basic "rightness" of an action is considered. At stage five, a long-run point of view involving self-respect and the greater good of the community is developed.
>
> At stage six, the person becomes governed by very broad moral principles...

The preoccupation with "self" which has been necessary to arrive at this level of development now evaporates. With the achievement of dignity and self-realization, the individual has become virtually free of anxieties. Able now to view the world as a broad canvas, "The big picture," this person has become deeply experienced at separating fact from feeling.

How he or she "feels" about any situation now depends wholly upon what he or she *thinks* about that situation. Facts—the way things *are*—no longer generate frustrations. This person solves problems and accepts circumstances. Depression, the bugaboo of folks not fully self-developed, no longer exists.

Perhaps one of the most moving summations of this level of mental and emotional peace was written years ago by an unknown author; and adopted by Alcoholics Anonymous as "The A.A. Prayer:"

> "God, grant me the serenity to accept those things I cannot change...
>
> The courage to change the things I can...

And the wisdom to know the
difference."

The *courage* to solve *problems*...the *peace of mind* to accept *circumstances* ...and the *thinking ability* to tell one from the other...

The reader is, right now, at some point in development between level one and level six. He or she may have experienced a sensation of *deja vue*; of having seen or experienced these concepts already. Some of this will seem rather elementary (I knew *that*) while other thoughts require the reader to slow down and ponder meanings.

That's all good: Because what you are NOW going to do is take a searching and fearless personal inventory. Before you continue to the concluding pages of this book, take the time to carefully analyze where you, personally, fit into the concepts you've been reading. The importance of taking this orientation/inventory simply cannot be overstated: In the many years Dr. Bob has worked with people, not one of them has achieved mental self-sufficiency if this step was neglected or done carelessly. Nobody failed to improve his or her well-being when this vital assessment was properly done.

Find a place where you can be alone for an extended time, a place with as few distractions as possible. Take a notebook and pencil(s) with you and write about yourself. Be brutally frank and honest: Nobody except you (at this point) will see what you are writing.

Inventory *facts* about your emotional development:

—How often do I find myself engaged in an activity I've done before; one which was followed by feelings of guilt or shame or self-reproach?

—Do people seek me out as a confidant? How well do I *really* know how to listen to others?

—Is it difficult for me to think "cooly and calmly;" or do I become very emotional while trying to solve problems?

—Am I usually concerned with others' welfare, or am I *usually* more interested in my own gain?

—Can I honestly claim to know the difference between feelings and thinking? How does my conscious relate to my subconscious? Am I *aware* of my subconscious; can my cognitive mind actually perceive my conative mind as a distinct entity?

—Do other people seem to "like" me? Do I usually like them?

—How important is it that others approve of me? Do I allow my concern for acceptance to sway my thinking away from what I genuinely believe in?

—Am I a conformist? —Is it because I consciously *want* to conform; or am I afraid of the consequences if I don't?

—If I am a noncomformist, is it because I am guided by moral precepts and principles, or am I simply a rebel without a cause? Am I "different" because I am disgusted with conformist society, or because I intend to *improve the quality* of society, no matter how significant my contributions? (Am I—honestly—part of the solution...or part of the problem?)

—Which emotions are more familiar:
Jealousy or affection...?
"I want" or generosity...?
Anger or compassion...?
Self-reproach or self-respect?

—If causasian, and a black family wanted to buy a home near mine, would I be concerned about what would happen to the value of my property...or would I be concerned about that family's rights: To be here, and to pursue happiness...?

—If I had as much income as I want, would it bring me peace of mind?

The inventory should not be limited to what you've seen here; these thoughts are "starters." Plan to spend many hours in *deep* thought about the quality of life in general. List as many attributes as you can possibly think of which, taken together, would "create" the kind of person you would regard most highly...and then rate your own self.

It's helpful to make two separate lists on each topic; one list for how you *feel* about yourself and another stating as factually as possible what you *think* about yourself.

This orientation/inventory is intended to provide you with answers to three generalized questions. The questions are general; the answers should be as specific and wide-ranging as you can possibly make them.

Question one: Where am I "Coming from?" What kind of background have I? Was my family modest or prominent? Did my childhood prepare me to be emotionally able to cope with life? Do I have a solid education? As I progressed from childhood into adult life, what were my personal assets...and liabilities?

Question two: Where am I today? —Given my age and background, how have I progressed toward emotional maturity? Am I *relatively* satisfied with my development, or am I suffering from self-disgust? (re-read "Please Hear What I'm NOT Saying"—is that you?) What are my *present* personality/emotional strong points; what are my weaknesses?

Question three: Where do I want to go? In the broadest terms, define the personal qualities you wish to achieve over the long haul. Remember not to become sidetracked by trying to modify your personality characteristics. We are looking for the qualities of maturity which fit your own personality. If by now you still wish the 180-Degree Theory would turn a quiet, thoughtful, analytical person into everyone's party-time favorite, you have a *long* way to go in search of emotional maturity. In such a hopeless (and useless) ambition as that, you'd do better consulting Dr. Jekyll and Mr. Hyde instead of Dr. Nara and Mr. Mariner.

How you should "feel" about your personality was summed up in a recent popular book-title: "I'm OK — You're OK" (And that's OK, too.)

1. Where am I *coming from?*
2. Where am I *now?*
3. Where am I *going?*

Complete the inventory—the orientation—and then we'll chart the course.

Chapter Thirteen

"The Shortest Distance Between Two Points"

Somewhere between "Math One" and differential calculus most of us were told that the shortest distance between two points is a straight line. Having discovered where you are now (point A) and where you want to go (point X), the fastest way to get there is to head directly for point X, right?

—Ask Christopher Columbus about the 180-Degree Theory. Just as the world is round and frequently the quickest way to go south is to head due north, we discover that sometimes the shortest distance between two points in emotional maturity is *not* a stright line.

In fact, if you want to get *really* exotic, the astronauts would cheefully explain that the further away point X is from your starting point, the more your course *must* curve: A straight line would never connect two points in deep inter-stellar space.

More practically: If your objective of self-realization is a long way off, you probably don't have enough experience and familiarity with the terrain to make a "quantum leap." Moses and his people wandered for fourty years in the desert going from captivity to the promised land: You can make the same trip today as an afternoon's outing.

Don't become anxious about how long it takes you to arrive at your mental destination. You have spent this much of your life wandering aimlessly, trusting to luck, society, and a little help from your friends to "do right''' by you. Now you are preparing to take charge of your mental destiny.

Super! But you *are not yet* an experienced navigator. Steve Mariner once skippered a boat from Pensacola to Key West, Florida. The quickest way to do this, of course, is to steer a course across the Gulf of Mexico directly from point A to point B. Had he done so, he might not have lived to help write this book: At best, he'd have suffered the ego-battering of being hauled ashore; out of fuel, lost, and drifting.

The courses, for those who are boat buffs, were 118° to Cedar Key (from St. George Island), 175° to Clearwater, "follow the shore" to Naples, and 185° to to Key West. The *best* course (not necessarily the quickest) from Pensacola to Key West, for the circumstances prevailing, was *not* a straight line.

Set your mind's-eye on your *goals* in life, and call this Point X. Make the goals as high as you can reasonably expect to achieve; this is the worst possible time to let your feelings cheat you by minimizing what you "deserve" out of life.

Then, once you have a firm "fix" on where you want to end up, begin to analyze the intermediate points; the more attainable Points B and C and D...

We've made mental/emotional maturity level six, for example, something very desirable for anyone. If you are, now, a level two, then for heaven's sake work on level three (point B). Level six is Point X, and *you don't know how to get there*—not yet, not without the experience and confidence you'll attain while working toward the next level.

If you're shy, and don't want to be, the worst thing you could do would be to set out tomorrow morning thinking you can become a total convert in one day. Start by saying "hi" to the elevator operator where you work, or ask the gas station attendant his name. *Act less shy;* the feelings will catch up shortly. Asking the gas-pumper his name is something you can *do,* and the activity will decrease the feelings of shyness. *Acting your way to a new feeling* means performing actions *you can handle.* Demanding an interview with Johnny Carson is *not* a cure for shyness. (It may be Point X, if you're an interviewer/journalist; the man in the filling station, however, is Point B. Go there first.)

Incidentally, in the illustration above, if a shy person demanded an interview with Johnny Carson it would be an excellent demonstration of *feeling your way to a new action:* It may make emotional sense and give the person a "gutsy" feeling: It won't work and the shyness is further reinforced.

Perhaps the best "next step" for everyone is to determine his or her specific type. Review the chapter outlining these types and characteristics, and then get some help from family and/or associates.

Ask people to "rate" you on the two scales; assertiveness and expressiveness. It's a good idea to think up some "situational" questions rather than topical questions: For example, rather than asking people if they would rate you more quiet, or more outspoken, ask instead questions such as, "Do I usually gesture noticeably, or do I seldom use my hands expressively?"

Find out how bluntly-spoken people think you are...whether you're more concerned with planning or with doing...whether you seem usually concerned about others' feelings or are, instead, generally not all that sensitive.

Watch out for your own self-concepts while you're doing this. By all means, rate yourself; but don't be too surprised if others will see you differently than you see yourself. The importance of getting help with this analysis is evident: On our own, we are more likely than not to make some "bad guesses," and the *objective* is to discover our *real* personality style.

You'll find that you tend more toward one style than the others: You are either

A. A Pusher
B. An Outspoken
C. A Sensitive
D. An Examiner

Once you've pegged yourself, study *carefully* the profile sketch for your personality. Think about past experiences which are examples of being pushed out of your personal comfort stage into reaction stage (two) and over-reaction stage (three). The goal is to become intimately familiar with *your own* emotional signals which will tell you when you are slipping over the edge into activity you wouldn't do in comfort stage one.

As long as you remain in stage one, you can think with your cognitive mind. The further you go into stages two and three, the more the emotions will control your activities.

Almost always when we begin to slip out of our comfort zone *and are aware of it,* we can prevent it from happening. A pusher, for example, can remain in stage one even though an examiner is wasting his time with a long-winded explanation of the background to a problem...*if he realizes what's happening.*

Wasting his time and being bogged down in procedure will trigger a pusher's emotions. Sensing that he is beginning to get uncomfortable, the pusher can "take hold" of himself and say to himself something like, "Okay...I don't *like* this, but it won't take forever. Charlie, there, is doing the best he can—but he's not like me. Therefore, *I will listen* to Charlie—as comfortably as possible—whether my feelings like it or not."

As you become more and more familiar with your own personality, begin analyzing those around you. It's more than just "fun," being able to type-cast and predict others' actions. It is a dynamically-potent method of reinforcing your self-understanding. Becoming adept at synchronizing your speaking and listening methods, your body English and actions, with those of another person of a different personality, will give you insights to yourself you never dreamed of.

More than that: Being able to maintain the *other* person's comfort zone without losing your own "cool" will help you become extraordinarily proficient at relating with others.

You'll know you are doing well, indeed, when members of all three other personality types agree that you are articulate, competent, and comfortable to deal with.

Your own personality quirks are the residence of your feelings, your emotions. They are *most comfortable* when at home, naturally. However: They can learn how to conduct themselves while "visiting" *someone else's house!* No, you can't—and shouldn't—try to change what you are. But you *can* "act" differently, sometimes for prolonged periods, without any mental or emotional strain. *Knowing you are doing it* (cognition) keeps the feelings (conative process) in check. There is no discomfort; it is, in fact, usually enjoyable and always challenging, interesting.

On the home front, understanding your own personality needs and those of other family members can contribute to peace and harmony. This is the *wrong* place to "act" out of character; here, instead, each member should understand the other's style and "bend" to meet it.

If your wife/husband is a sensitive, you can make that life a bright place by realizing that the human relationships in the household are the one more important element than any other. To "use" this knowledge *against* a sensitive—to manipulate the sensitive's concern for other people's feelings—would be a disgusting perversion of this knowledge. No emotionally-mature person would consider such an obscene action.

If your spouse is a pusher—and you're not—you can add a measure of wellbeing to your household simply by remembering how time-oriented, goal-oriented and un-expressive this person usually is. You needn't try to live *your* life as if you were a pusher—you can't—but you can do it *occasionally* when the circumstances warrant; and you can *remain aware* all of the time about the other party's personality/emotional needs.

If one of you is an outspoken, you can use the same techniques. If *both* of you are outspokens...well...perhaps you could draw straws or make up a schedule regarding which has front stage center...and when? Seriously: Two outspokens sharing a life could be, and should be, colorful, dynamic and filled with love.

Carry this "game" with you to your occupation, and you will be amazed at how those around you, with whom you formerly "had trouble," suddenly seem more likeable. Did *they* change? No...but you did. The more this method becomes a subconscious, automatic reaction to others around you, the more it will pay huge dividends both personally and professionally.

Notice, again, that the self-interest aspect is not an unhealthy, "selfish" technique to help you gain ascendancy over others. The more you help yourself become personality self-realized, the more others can relate to you. You become the person others confide in. You "have a knack" for making them more comfortable.

Of *course* you benefit...and so does everyone else. Again, that's that kind of "game" 180-Degree players prefer: Everybody wins.

Now you begin in earnest learning to *act your way to a new feeling.* The concepts related to the cognitive (conscious), conative (subconscious) and autonomous minds need to be studied carefully. You've identified areas of your own shortcomings in interpersonal relationships. You can *thoughtfully* analyze the way you perform numerous actions which ought to be amended.

You can use your mind to create images of yourself performing the actions the way you *want* to. Once you've developed a clear mental image of yourself performing these new actions; the "way you want to be," simply begin *acting* in the new way.

Don't push yourself too far, too quickly. Your feelings will backfire immediately when you begin breaking new ground. When emotions tell you, "Man, I *know damn well* I can't do that!"—That's a tough preconception to overcome, and failing at it will reinforce the mind-set that "you can't do it." Instead, choose a related area of your life or personal qualities and work at this until you've overcome your feeling's objections.

"Hey, baby...I don't know if you can handle that," would be a good place to start. Just square off the shoulders, get a solid mental image of how you are going to *act* —and start acting: "Sure I can. Here we go..."

Each successful performance of the "acting your way to a new feeling" technique re-programs the subconscious with positive mental images about yourself. Just as surely as a lifetime of habit can "set" negative feelings into place and constantly reinforce them, creating new habits can turn these into positive feelings and equally reinforce *them.*

Steve Mariner formerly drove beat-up old cars, on their last legs. The interior usually was littered with discarded plastic coffee-cups; the outside so dirty the original color was anybody's guess. The car was what his feelings told him he "deserved," and he treated the car the way *it* deserved.

The *last* old car he had was a decrepit Dodge sedan. The paint was oxidized and ugly and it had so many miles on it the odometer had given up in disgust. There was one difference, now:

Steve acted differently toward that old Dodge, which he affectionately named "Old Angina" —heart-ache. The engine got fresh oil and new spark plugs on a regular schedule; the interior was kept clean. Steve told himself, "I am going to *act as though* I'm driving a shiny, late-model Cadillac."

What would you guess Steve is driving, today...? —That's right; in this minor aspect of his life as in many major ways, he learned how to act his way to a few feeling about what he "deserved" —and, like old Shakespeare said, "...it then follows like the night follows the day..."

The old car illustration above makes another point,

one of value: We begin acting our way out of where we are *now*. If you wait for the newer car before you act like you ought to be driving it, it may be a long time coming...

Our personal lives, our emotions, our lifestyles and our possessions all have one common meeting point *today:* Together, they make up our starting point. Begin with what you have, and begin acting your way toward what you want. You are *not* going to immediately jump to Point X: You are going to act your way from point A to point B to point C...and on and on...until you arrive *securely* at your destination; and without the slightest mental reservation as to whether you deserve to be there.

Chapter Fourteen

"Take Me Along"

Some years back an airline commercial was based on the theme, "Take me along." The idea was that travelers could take their spouses with them at reduced airfares. The commercial hinted that peace, love and joy would reign supreme because husband and wife could now "fly united;" no pun, slur, off-key joke or reference to United Air Lines intended.

It was a good idea for the airline.

It is an absolute necessity for a 180-Degree player.

We have seen lives so profoundly changed by these concepts that the person quite literally became someone else, someone at the same time still "himself," but so dynamically different in maturity and personal qualities there seemed to be even a shifting in physical appearance.

One such person sat across the table for hours from a person who had known him well and was not recognized. There is no doubt that the effectiveness of the 180-degree theory can almost make someone over "from scratch."

That, of course, is part of it's benefit. It contains, however, the seeds for a different form of personal disaster. Please don't assume that your spouse won't react to the changes you'll go through. All of us fear the unknown and accept the familiar. If you love your spouse, please make certain that the two of you embark on your 180-degree course *together.*

There can be no more rewarding experience than watching each other grow and become more emotionally-secure. Problems which have taken away from happiness begin to "go away" as your intermingled personal relationship becomes more mature. The potential for helping each other is almost limitless. There is something about this method of self-help which seems to spontaneously generate *un*-selfishness.

Each of you will find yourself more concerned with helping your partner than with your own progress. In itself, this is a warmly-rewarding concept; but the "frosting on the cake" is that *the more you try to give this knowledge away, the faster you attain it.*

Years ago, as Dr. Bob Nara's mastery of these concepts began to bring him financial, personal and emotional success on a scale beyond the wildest imaginings of his immigrant grandparents, the relationship with Ruth Nara became strained.

Had he not realized what was happening and, in a sense, "gone back after" his wife, perhaps their marriage would not have survived.

The story of what happened then, when both Bob and Ruth pioneered the 180-Degree compass heading, is a narrative of development from lower emotional maturity to higher levels. It is a heart-warming story, and it is Ruth's story; so we will let her tell it, from the pages of *Feelings:*

> Bob asked me to contribute some of my thoughts and feelings to you—those that I hope might be helpful to you in your life.
>
> My husband is my very best friend—He is my mirror who gives me honest and open feedback. I feel I can and do talk to him about anything. I trust him completely and I truly believe in what he is trying to do in this world. I feel honored that he has

included me in the sharing of these goals which are quite simple...to help make this world a little better place to live.

This relationship didn't happen overnight and it wasn't always a bed of roses. For a period of time it was quite a bumpy road. I think one of my biggest problems that I had to overcome in our marriage, and I see many people struggling with this today, is the fight for control. One of the ways that Bob helped me overcome this was to gently force me out of the home (when the kids were a little older) and into the office with him.

Once I began to experience and share his everyday problems and relate to them, he became even more sympathetic to mine. This was a key factor in helping us become far closer as a couple.

It is awfully easy to stop learning, somewhere partway through life—to get caught up in the same habits and patterns that are comfortable but hold us in a self-made prison.

Once I broke out of my rut and began to learn again, it felt good and I wanted more. The learning, to a large degree, was about myself. Who am I? What am I here for? Where am I going? A friend from Chicago invited us to an encounter being held in his home. It was an unbelievable experience for both of us. The encounter increased our awareness about ourselves and our relationship with some others...but not all. Some relationships tended to dissolve to nothing. (Generally, relationships require efforts from both parties to maintain them. Without this effort, relationships tend to break down.)

As we worked closer together and we related better and better, it is amazing how my values and priorities changed. THINGS were far less important to me now and feelings and people were far more important.

Materialism is a big item in our society and love for others...and caring...is practically non-existent. I began to wonder what else society had taught me that might be a big fraud.

I became increasingly aware that our relationship—Bob's and mine—was the most important aspect of my life. My children were very important, but they were growing up and would soon be off on their own. In fact, that was part of our responsibility to them: To help them become independent of us.

Our oldest is now a freshman in college and the two younger ones will be college age in three more short years. I find this easy to accept now that I am completely involved with my husband. This probably wouldn't be true if I had stayed in my rut.

I was always a quiet, rather introverted person but lately I can say I feel far more secure and confident in my abilities as a human being. Over the past several years, I have helped my husband give lecture programs here and there around the country and overseas. This is quite an accomplishment for me because I almost fainted from fright when I gave my first speech in college.

I really feel that I have changed completely and I attribute 90% of the reason to my husband's concern for me and his efforts to help me. He was changing and I didn't want to get left behind. It was either a question of paying the price or perhaps experiencing a broken marriage or God knows what. I chose to pay the price and believe me it has reaped untold rewards for us. Life is exciting, it is never dull. There is so much to be done!

We've learned to make valuable use of our time. Do the most important thing first, eliminate the unimportant. We work hard; the kids work, too.

Bob has been a great father to our children, something that I think is rare in our society today. Some of the qualities that make him a good father in my opinion are his commonsense, his feelings for others, his ability to make decisions and to allow others around him freedom to make decisions.

I have a feeling that all fathers (at some point in their lives) would like to be great fathers or at least, better fathers. This thought I learned in the encounter, that I hadn't thought about before:

There are no perfect people. We are all at some point in our development (we are enroute). Since many of us only use about ten percent of our potential abilities, we could all improve if we had the desire and know-how. Up until now, there has been very little, if any, mechanism in society for personal growth. Just recently, we renewed acquaintances with a person we hadn't seen for 20 years...he had changed so little mentally, we could have been apart seemingly less than a week!

This never ceases to amaze me. This person is now divorced and remarried, so growth never came through his relationship. From our experience, I feel the husband-wife relationship is a valuable place for growth...and it takes growth to achieve love.

I have always put most all my efforts into pleasing and helping my husband. I cook him nourishing and tasty things to eat (we both watch the calories, but love to eat), make our sexual life interesting (this always pleases a husband) and give him lots of support whenever and wherever possible.

We had some close friends that lived near us and who were having a rough time of it in their marriage. The husband confided to Bob and asked his help several times when his wife left him. They would live apart for a while, until they would manage to get together for a time...and back and forth.

One fall Friday evening he was killed in a lone-car accident coming home on the road he knew so well. His wife was completely devestated. To this day she feels guilty that she didn't try harder to please and help him. Now, it is: "If I only did this differently...and if I hadn't done that..."

I think she would tell us all—now—that we'd better take good care of each other.

You can't be half-pregnant...life is a matter of total commitment.

——Ruth Nara

The reader may infer, from Ruth's obvious love and respect for Dr. Bob, that their marriage relationship is lopsided; that Dr. Bob is an object of her hero-worship. The message comes through loud and clear: Ruth doesn't believe she would have "made it" without her husband.

Is it a one-sided affair? Once a close friend asked Dr. Bob if he could have done as well on his own, without Ruth's support. His reply:

"...without Ruth? —Maybe. Probably. Sure, I guess so—for what, for God's sake? It isn't something *I* did *for* her: We did it together...it isn't 'my' life, or hers—it's ours."

If you have decided to take a trip on the 180-Degree Airline, remember the all-important commercial: "Take me along..."

If you start out alone, you might end up alone. Although your personal life can be extremely successful either way, think about Dr. Bob's reply:

"...for what, for God's sake?"

Chapter Fifteen

'Thoughts on Paying the Price'

In the last chapter, Ruth Nara mentioned "paying the price" for a fully self-realized lifestyle. What did she mean by that?

We've often heard it said, "There ain't no such thing as a free lunch." Sooner or later in life, you get what you pay for...and you pay for what you get.

Learning and implementing the concepts making up the 180-Degree Theory is *hard work*. There will be perhaps as many periods of frustrated failure as there are peaks of exhilarating success. Taking the good with the bad is a way of life, and there is nothing in the 180-Degree Theory that can insulate you from blind fortune: "The slings and arrows" life throws at us from time to time.

As you become more and more adept at maturing emotionally, others will notice the success-orientation of your life. Make no mistake, they won't all be pressing forward to congratulate you. Ruth Nara spoke of friends and friendships that simply "went away" as she and Bob became concept-oriented instead of "thing-oriented."

As you prepare to bring these ideas into your own life, we want to give you fair warning about how some others will react to the new elements of your life and lifestyle...and to give you a challenge, because it *is* worth it.

The famous Dr. William C. Menninger, before he

died, left a legacy of psychological knowledge that has made this world a better—at least, better-understood—place for many.

Dr. Menninger's "Criteria of Emotional Maturity" gives us a quick reference about what we are striving *for:*

> Having the ability to deal constructively with reality.
>
> Having the capacity to adapt to change.
>
> Having a relative freedom from symptoms that are produced by tensions and anxieties.
>
> Having the capacity to find more satisfaction in giving than in receiving.
>
> Having the capacity to relate to other people in a consistent manner with mutual satisfaction and helpfulness.
>
> Having the capacity to sublimate; to direct one's hostile (primitive) energy into creative and constructive outlets.
>
> Having the capacity to love.
>
> ——William C. Menninger
> 1899 — 1966

Keeping this in mind, we will share a story about life and its criticism, and the all-too-frequent response evoked by success:

> One year when I was superintendent of schools we had an undefeated football team, and as the season progressed we started getting a lot of static from some of our jealous

competitors. Incidentally, I have never known a losing team to be investigated. The situation got so bad that our football team and student body began fighting back through the newspaper columns and other means at their disposal. Finally, we called a special assembly to talk about the situation. I told them:

There are two kinds of administrative problems that go along with athletic teams. You have one kind of problem when you are winning, and another kind when you are losing. You have very real problems either way.

Now, personally, I prefer the problems that go along with success. The kind of problems we have right now are the kind I would choose. If I had my "druthers," I would "druther" have this kind.

When you are successful, your enemies howl to high heaven. You must expect that. But let me caution you not to expect too much enthusiasm from your friends either.

Do not become embittered about human nature if your friends don't get out the brass band to celebrate your successes in life. Remember this: Your friends usually like to see you do well—but not *too* well. Our team is undefeated and unscored on. That's "too well" for a lot of folks to swallow. So some people are saying some nasty things about us. And some of our friends, who should be standing up for us, are not doing it.

Now one of the "problems" of success is: What should we do about

> it? To answer that question is the purpose of our meeting. May I suggest first to you squad members, and to the whole student body, that you put these critics down as people who sincerely appreciate your superiority?
>
> Let's give them credit for that. A person just can't be jealous of another whom he knows is not doing as well as he is. You can't do that if you try.
>
> So first you give your critics credit for recognizing your superiority. Next you mark the whole thing off your list and forget it. If you start throwing back their mud-balls, you won't be superior anymore. Booker T. Washington said one time, "One man can't hold another one down in the ditch without staying there with him."
>
> ——McFarland, *The Eloquence Of Public Speaking.*

So...you've been given some insight as to how others will react as you begin to seek—and receive—life more abundantly. Is it worth it? Now for the challenge, from the writings of the late President Theodore Roosevelt:

> It is not the critic who counts, not the man who points out how the strong man stumbled, or where the doer of deeds could have done them better.
>
> The credit belongs to the man who is actually in the arena; whose face is marred by dust and sweat and blood; who strives valiantly; who errs and comes short again and again; who knows the great enthusiasms, the great devotions, and spends himself in a worthy cause; who at the best knows

> in the end the triumph of high achievement; and who at the worst, if he fails, at least fails while daring greatly; so that his place shall never be with those cold and timid souls who know neither victory nor defeat.

Once you have dared and begun to win; and you've grown tall enough and have the inner courage to forgive your critics for being blind to their shortcomings while magnifying yours, there may be temptation to "make them pay" for giving you a rough time. You must never, never succumb to the temptation of winning by creating someone else's loss. To illustrate, a final quotation on success: This time from Dr. Bob, as it appeared in *Feelings:*

> In planning our efforts toward a successful future, another thing to keep in mind is that we must stick to a game where everybody wins. That may seem strange in this highly competitive world, but I believe it's true.
>
> Our society is geared today toward games where we have a winner and a loser. One only has to turn to the weekend television programs of football, from late morning steadily through early evening; each one a competitive battle that will result in a winner and a loser.
>
> I have never really liked the highly competitive realm because I generally lose either way: If I'm the winner, I feel badly about the other guy and if I lose, I naturally feel badly as all losers undoubtedly do.
>
> There is no such thing as a really good loser, so I like to concentrate on

games where everybody wins. This is possible, I believe, although it may require that one not get ahead as fast as he otherwise might...but when he does, it will give him better inner feelings and allow him to enjoy the fruits of his efforts without suffering the guilt feelings resulting from doing others in while we get ahead ourselves...

If we work it right, there is generally enough to go around for everybody.

——R. O. Nara, *Feelings*

"Paying the price" means learning how to respond to criticism. Whether active or passive; explicit or implied, criticism can evoke an immediate—often dangerous—emotional response: *"I'll show you..."* The frequent human reaction to "being put down" is to try to fight our way "back up." This is an invitation to "thinking with the emotions," and it can result in some of life's most awkward "backfires."

The winning football team a few pages ago had everything coming its way. The only true facts, in that situation, were all in that school's favor and even the problems, as the superintendent pointed out, were the kind he'd "druther" have.

Piqued by criticism they "didn't deserve," the students were beginning to lash back in revenge. The common emotion in that student body could be neatly summed up as, "we'll show them!"

Had that superintendent not been wise and articulate enough to see the approaching difficulty and ward it off, those young men and women would have been doomed to live out Booker T. Washington's ob-observation: You can't keep someone in the mud at the bottom of the ditch unless you join him...and stay there.

A certain amount of "I'll show them" in our lives can be beneficial. You can't become obsessed with "showing them" *anything* without becoming both determined and persistent. When determination and persistence are coupled to rational, unemotional thinking, the effect is almost irresistable.

If a stock boy overheard two company clerks talking about him, and their criticism stung him deeply, he might either "blow up" or "buckle down." (Notice that there is 180 degrees difference in those two expressions...)

"That kid in the stockroom is slow as a turtle," one clerk says, and the other chimes in: "Yeah...and he's not very bright, either."

That kid in the stockroom, being human, would want to "show them." Would he let the air out of their tires; would he put sugar in their cars' gas tanks...would he find some way related to the job to get these clerks in trouble with management?

Or would he suddenly become determined that he would be the best stockroom employee at Western Widgets, Inc?

The first way would give him no rational benefit; it would likely produce an emotional kickback of guilt, and if he got caught, he'd lose his job.

The other way of "showing" those clerks could result in promotion after promotion. In time, the senior vice-president of Western Widgets, Inc., would get a warm inner glow every time he walked through the stockroom: "I guess I showed *them!*"

"I'll show you!" can be either damaging or rewarding; and it is powerful either way. Perhaps the simplest distinction between the beneficial and the detrimental application of this emotive force would be this easy test:

If I show them, will I be trying to make someone lose...or will everybody win?

Once an executive with a major corporation was shocked when a promotion he expected went to another person. While nobody at the firm had been the least bit critical of his performance, his reaction was intensely emotional. His feelings screamed that he had been deeply criticized; that he hadn't got what he deserved.

"I'll show *them,*" he decided, and instantly an emotionally satisfying course of action came to mind. He spent the rest of the day composing his letter of resignation, giving the company thirty days notice.

He reasoned (not necessarily realistically) that the company would be forced to revise its opinion of him and to reconsider the promotion that was deservedly his.

A week went by, during which no reference was made to his resignation. "Ah," he thought, "I know that game. The old war of nerves, hey? Well, I'm Joe Cool. If they want to pretend, so will I. I'll bet they're *really* sweating it out..."

Near the end of the second week, Joe Cool had some misgivings. "They're testing me," he decided. "They just want to see if I've got what it takes to play the hard-ball game; if I'm tough enough to handle top management. Well, I'll show them: I'm not just Joe Cool, I'm Hardball Joe Cool.

Friday of the third week the general manager called him into the front office. He was politely given an opportnity to reconsider the resignation and keep his job; and just as politely—with massive dignity—Hardball Joe Cool told them he'd made up his mind.

Near the end of the fourth week he noticed one of the office staff going from desk to desk with a cigar box, apparently taking up a collection. His curiosity got the best of him when he, himself, was not approached. He called the secretary into his office and asked what it was all about.

"They're taking up a collection for you," she said.

"Aha!" Immediately he assumed he'd won; and his fellow employees were preparing to celebrate his promotion. He guessed they'd kept it from him all this time so they could announce it at a surprise party.

"Whose idea was it?" he asked her.

"The general manager's," she replied. "You know, Joe...he really liked you. He told his secretary he was sorry you were leaving. Can I ask you a question?"

Still stunned, Joe murmured, "Sure...go ahead."

"...Why *did* you quit? You had it made here..."

The hardest part was having to tell his wife that evening, and realizing that her reply was truly what he deserved, because he'd earned it:

"Old Hardball Joe Cool, eh? I guess you sure showed them, didn't you...?"

Epilog

Come with us to a plateau in the Libyan Sahara. As our all-terrain vehicle approaches, the fuselage of a B-24 stands out starkly against the flat reaches of sand: It is the only landmark on the horizon. The nearer we come, the more we are amazed at how well-preserved this aircraft is: She's been here, now, for...let's see... well over thirty years.

We can still read the numbers painted on her side: B-24-D-25-Co, Air Corps Ser. No. 41-24301. Her nickname is equally legible at the rounded nose of the fuselage. We've come to visit the *Lady Be Good.*

We go inside. Other than a fine coating of dust everywhere, the *Lady* seems almost alive and ready to fly; as soon as her crew comes back. Idly, without thinking, you pick up a stick of Spearmint chewing gum that was lying on the cockpit console; unwrap it and begin chewing.

The hairs at the back of your neck raise slightly and you feel the chill of goose-flesh as it comes home to you: The gum was on board this B-24 on the morning of April 4, 1943...and it is as fresh as if you just bought it this afternoon.

The story unfolds in your mind's-eye: Ten crewmen, bone-weary and frustrated from an aborted first mission, are bucking a ghost headwind as they return to Soluch airfield. Through gritty, red-rimmed eyes they peer downward through the night and haze, hoping for some sign they have finally crossed the Mediterranean and are over land.

The pilot reaches for a switch and energizes the radio, his hand passing within inches of the mute, inactive Automatic Direction Finder. He calles Benina Tower, adjacent to Soluch:

"Benina, this is Two Four Three Zero One; over."

"Three Zero One; Benina: Go ahead."

"Request inbound RDF check; over."

"Roger, Three Zero One. Key your mike for five seconds, please." The operator manipulates the loop antenna, and then goes back on the air:

"Three Zero One; Benina: You're inbound on three-three-zero, right on course. Over."

"Roger, Benina. Three Zero One, out."

Now you re-live, with those men, the mounting sense of danger as fuel levels drop lower and lower. One by one, the engines are cut and the props feathered, their blades turning head-on to the airflow to reduce drag. Finally the pilot keys the intercom: "Prepare to bail out; Mae Wests and survival gear. Sorry, you guys...it's gonna be a wet one."

The rest of the story flickers through your imagination: The shock of landing in the desert; the fruitless search for a comrade whose parachute failed...the discussion about where we are and what we should do...the final, unbelievable trek through eight days and seventy miles; burning by day and freezing by night, miraculously staying alive on one canteen-capful of water each day...

The ultimate, inevitable end, marked only by the final entry in the co-pilot's diary: "Monday, April 12. No help yet, very cold nite..."

180-Degree errors—assumptions—botched-up communications—false hopes—heartbreaking courage—faith defeating despair—Humanity in all of its greatness and weakness, with the hulk of the *Lady Be Good* an eternal monument and reminder.

You reach for the radio switch and flip it on. The hum of a vibrator startles you and then, as the tubes warm up, there is a faint hiss in the headset. Before you catch yourself, on an impulse, you key the microphone and say, "Benina Tower, this is Three Zero One; over."

"Go ahead, Three Zero One," comes a bored voice.

You almost whisper: "Benina, Three Zero One: Request inbound heading check."

Today's RDF equipment has no back-side-of-the-loop error, nor does an operator need to turn an antenna. The reply is almost instantaneous:

"Three Zero One, Benina: You're inbound on one five zero; right on. Over."

"Roger, Benina. Three Zero One out."

As you replace the microphone your eyes are drawn to the compass. The indicator is frozen on course 319 magnetic, where it has rested for more than thirty years. You do some quick arithmetic: If Benina tower says you are on a bearing of 150 relative to the tower, you have to be actually heading north if you're in-bound...that would be...let's see now, 180 plus 150... you'd be on 330, right?

And yet, the *Lady Be Good* was flying almost south when she crashed: She was flying course 150.

Slowly you figure it out. When she came down, the aircraft slid for several hundred feet on her belly. As she slowed to a stop, she must have turned almost a complete semi-circle.

With no human being touching her controls, the *Lady Be Good* seemed to have made one last, dying effort to finish Mission Number 109; she was trying to head for Soluch.

She almost made it through the full 180 degrees.

Postscript

The authors believe these concepts, the basic principles of the 180-Degree Theory, can help anyone achieve mental self-sufficiency. We have watched numerous people apply these concepts in their own lives, invariably improving them and usually enabling them to achieve mental and emotional well-being.

We have carefully shared our belief that there is no true material success in life without first arriving at a personal set of values and emotional relationships on an inner level. Not surprisingly, we firmly believe that to attempt to improve our lives in a material way without first becoming mentally and emotionally self-sufficient is, in itself, an example of "the back side of the loop" in the 180-Degree Theory.

Material success first, with concern for inner success relegated to second place, may seem attractive. It has, before, for thousands...perhaps millions...who achieved "success" only to die broken by life, in the end crippled by inner failure.

By no means do Nara and Mariner imply that material advantages in life have no value. We merely urge that the reader firmly fix his priorities—that he or she make mental self-sufficiency the primary goal.

Many, if not all, of the ideas making up the 180-Degree Theory can be applied equally as well in the pursuit of material achievement as they apply in the pursuit of happiness. In fact, some 180-Degree principles lend themselves to specific methods of achieving external values in life.

We have included little or no information designed for the improvement of material status, in this book, because we realized that to mix our message—to talk about inner well-being and external welfare together—would weaken the effectiveness of the message.

There is a sequel to the 180-Degree Theory. It's title is *Get Rich HELL...Get Well!* It is a "cook-book" containing recipes on how to do it; a prescription for attaining a healthy material status. It is based on the belief that there are far more people who would like to achieve financial and material security than there are those hoping to learn the secret of making a fortune.

Achieving great wealth without breaking the law or being incredibly lucky is almost impossible, unless there is first a secure foundation. To most of us, daydreams about fortune must eventually confront the reality that we are struggling just to keep even. Bills, mortgages, spiraling inflation and sometimes plummeting incomes should be our concern, not making a million dollars.

If the 180-Degree Theory has made sense to you; if you are now beginning to think in newer concepts and to view your life from an altered frame of reference, we believe you will agree with our basic premise: You don't need, just yet, to concern yourself with becoming rich. You'd much rather just get well.

We sincerely hope you will, now and for the immediate future, invest your concentration and efforts on mastering the 180-Degree Theory, learning how to make it work for you in improving the quality of your mental, emotional inner self. We'd like you to become mentally self-sufficient; to achieve wellbeing no matter what your material circumstances.

Then, when you feel (and think!) you are ready, perhaps it's time for *Get Rich Hell.* We want to help you, if you'll let us, because we want to be your friend; and a friend:

...is someone who leaves you with
all of your freedoms intact;
but obliges you to be fully what you are
...and to become all you can be.

Good luck, and God love you,

Bob Nara, Ruth Nara and Steve Mariner

ORAMEDICS INTERNATIONAL PRESS was established in 1978 by Oramedics International when it became apparent that most U.S. publishing houses avoid books which are either controversial or of relatively lesser commercial value, no matter how beneficial publication would be as a contribution to mankind.

Since its inception O.I. Press has published books and manuals which have established their value both in benefits to those who have read them and in the marketplace: People buy them.

A partial list of publications:

Money By The Mouthful

An expose of the dental profession with information about dental disease and its prevention.

How To Become Dentally Self-Sufficient

A lay person's "cookbook" of self-administered dental care—How to avoid disease and apply "first aid" to problems caused by prior disease. Save thousands of dollars in dentist bills.

The 180° Theory

How to become mentally self-sufficient; a self-help guide to coping with life and developing lasting peace of mind.

Get Rich Hell, Get Well!

A step-by-step method of becoming financially independent. *Not* just another get-rich-quick scheme (get rich, hell!) —this book helps the reader achieve financial health...to get "well."

What Makes Johnny Run

An overview of the psychology of individual dentists and of organized dentistry as a whole.

Feelings: Having an Encounter With Yourself

The publication which prompted *The 180° Theory*; considered by many an essential companion to *The 180° Theory:* A workbook-format to help develop personal mental and emotional growth.

The Psychology of Credit and Collections in Dental Practice

How to extend credit and collect payment easily without creating ill-will; written for dentists, beneficial to many professions.

Building Positive Mental Attitude in Dental Practice

A guide to coping with the emotional stress of this mentally-damaging profession.

Research Advocates Oramedics

A concise, but thorough, analysis of dental disease (odontosis) and Oramedics International's preventive approaches. Includes all known applicable research through early 1979. All statements documented in complete bibliography.

Applied Oramedics for Health Care Professionals

A step-by-step method for any member of the health care field to help patients and clients overcome and prevent dental disease (odontosis).

Changing Idealism Into Realism

The "Big Book" of Oramedics (for dentists): How to establish and maintain a preventive dental practice. Its 3-ring binder format allows constant updates and revisions. (Sold only upon approval of Oramedics International.)

* * *

Numerous brochures and pamphlets are available for use by dentists and the public, covering almost any topic in preventive (medical and self-help) dentistry; oral health care.

* * *

SOON TO COME: *Wounded Women;* a study of women emotionally crippled, victimized by bad marriages. Self-help guide to discovering the problems (and causes) in a damaging marriage; how to recover your own personality and regain emotional health.

* * *

A postcard to Oramedics International Press, 200 East Montezuma Ave., Houghton, MI 49931, will bring an up-to-date list of titles in print and current price information. *If you can't find the title you want in your bookstore* it can be ordered direct from O.I. Press.

One more thought:

There is no random human behavior...

Every action has purpose —conscious or unconscious; from thought or emotion —unless the person is demented.

We *think*...or we *feel*...then we act.

We either "drive" —or we're driven!